Family Planning

A Comedy

Frank Vickery

A SAMUEL FRENCH ACTING EDITION

SAMUEL
FRENCH
FOUNDED 1830

SAMUELFRENCH-LONDON.CO.UK
SAMUELFRENCH.COM

FAMILY PLANNING is fully protected under the copyright laws of the British Commonwealth, including Canada, the United States of America, and all other countries of the Copyright Union. All rights, including professional and amateur stage productions, recitation, lecturing, public reading, motion picture, radio broadcasting, television and the rights of translation into foreign languages are strictly reserved.

ISBN 978-0-573-01685-1

www.samuelfrench-london.co.uk

www.samuelfrench.com

FOR AMATEUR PRODUCTION ENQUIRIES

UNITED KINGDOM AND WORLD EXCLUDING NORTH AMERICA
plays@SamuelFrench-London.co.uk
020 7255 4302/01

Each title is subject to availability from Samuel French,

depending upon country of performance.

FAMILY PLANNING

First produced at the Dolman Theatre, Newport on 23rd March 1981 and subsequently at the Fortune Theatre, London on 9th August 1987, with the following cast of characters:

Gran	Christine Tuckett
Tracy	Lorraine John
Elsie	Lynfa Williams
Maisie Millard	Iris Griffiths
Jeffrey	Damian Townsend
Idris	Kelvin Lawrence-Jones
Bobby	Brian Meadows

The play directed by Brian Meadows
Designed by The Parc & Dare Theatre Company

The action of the play passes in the living-room, bedroom and hallway of a terraced house

ACT I   Thursday, 9.45 a.m.
ACT II   Later, the same evening
ACT III   Late morning, the following day

Time: the present

ACT I

A composite set. A living-room, bedroom and hallway. Thursday 9.45 a.m.

The living-room is the largest acting area and takes up two-thirds of the stage. The furniture is not modern—it should look well-worn but comfortable. There is an armchair L. Behind is a dining-table with three chairs. At the back of the set is a sideboard. This should be of the same type of wood as the table. To the right of the sideboard is the doorway which leads into the kitchen. DR is a two-seater settee. This should be positioned so that half of it is in the living-room area and the other half is in front of Gran's bedroom. The purpose of this is to extend the acting area of the living-room. Gran's bedroom needn't be more than 8 ft by 8 ft. The bed occupies the centre of her room. The wallpaper should have a faded pink flower design. On the wall above Gran's bed is a tapestry which reads "God is Love" or something of that sort. To the left of the bed is a small table. On it are three or four dirty mugs, a pack of well-used playing cards, orange peel, a clock and a piggy bank. To the right of the bed is a chair. On the back of this hangs Gran's handbag. The hallway is the smallest area with a front door and a small doorway leading upstairs. To the right of the front door is a hallstand with a mirror

If staging facilities permit the bedroom may be positioned on a higher level with practical stairs

When the CURTAIN *rises Gran is, as always, in bed. She is halfway through peeling an orange. Elsie is in the living-room, ironing. Tracy is sitting in the armchair with her leg over the arm. She is a rather tarty-looking teenager, wearing tight jeans, no bra and with two "love bites" on her neck. She browses through a magazine then looks up at Elsie uneasily. Gran by this time has finished peeling her orange and starts to eat it. Suddenly she spits something into her hand*

Gran Bloody pips!

Tracy bites her bottom lip, then speaks hesitantly

Tracy Mam?

Elsie continues ironing and replies without looking up

Elsie Mmmm?

Tracy (*having second thoughts*) Nothing, it's all right. (*She tries to read the magazine again but cannot concentrate. She speaks to Elsie once more*) Mam?

Elsie What?

Tracy (*after a slight pause*) How young were you when you got married?
Elsie (*freezing, then looking at Tracy*) Why?
Tracy (*trying to cover up*) Oh, nothing. I just wondered, that's all.
Elsie I was *too* young. I was nineteen. I was tricked.
Tracy (*laughing*) Tricked?
Elsie Your father told me he had some incurable disease and didn't expect to see the month out. That was in nineteen fifty-three.
Tracy He was a bit of a hypochondriac even then, was he?
Elsie A bit of one? He was fully fledged at the age of thirteen. I remember your gran telling me that he wanted to join the library when he was ten, and when he did, he didn't come home with Enid Blyton's Famous Five or anything like that, but George Newnes' Home Doctor.
Tracy The sign of things to come.
Elsie (*having stopped ironing momentarily*) I hope you haven't got any ideas about getting married, have you?
Tracy (*trying to laugh*) No.
Elsie That's all right then. I mean, I've got nothing against that boy you're going out with Tracy, but . . .
Tracy Bobby.
Elsie Bobby, yes. I've got nothing against him but he's . . . well he's . . .
Tracy Go on, tell me.
Elsie Well, he's no John Travolta, is he?
Tracy Dad was no Robert Redford either.
Elsie True. (*She stops and gazes into mid-air for a moment remembering*) He was more like . . . Paul Newman. (*She accidentally touches her hand with the iron and jumps*)
Tracy I can't think of anyone less like Paul Newman than Daddy.
Elsie Oh, he was good-looking—(*as an afterthought*)—when he was younger.
Tracy There's nothing wrong with Bobby.
Elsie I didn't say there was anything wrong with him Tracy, I was just saying that he's . . . he's . . . well, he's ugly that's all.
Tracy (*a little hurt*) Looks aren't everything.
Elsie No, I know. But they're a hell of a lot when you haven't got anything else.
Tracy I know he's not handsome—but it's not his looks I'm attracted to.
Elsie Oh, I'm afraid to ask the next question.
Tracy It's something I can't quite put my finger on.
Elsie Oh, my God.
Gran (*calling*) Elsie? Elsie?
Elsie Here she goes again. (*She goes out into the hall and shouts up the stairs to Gran*)

Tracy goes off into the kitchen

Gran Elsie?
Elsie What do you want?
Gran It's quarter to ten.
Elsie I know that Mam, I've just put the kettle on.

Gran I 'ave my cocoa at 'alf-past nine and it's quarter to ten.
Elsie I said I know Mam. I've just put the kettle on.
Gran Elsie?
Elsie (*exasperated*) What?
Gran It's quarter to ten.
Elsie (*screaming*) All right, all right. (*She goes back to the living-room*) She's starting her bloody nonsense again. If she doesn't have things to time, she screams blue murder.
Gran She's talking about me down there, I know she is.
Elsie Put the kettle on will you Trace?
Tracy (*off*) I'm just doing it.
Elsie (*resuming ironing*) She's getting to me this morning.
Gran I don't know why she doesn't put me in a home and finish with it.
Elsie I don't know why I don't put her in a home and finish with it.

Tracy enters

Tracy You wouldn't do that, would you Mam?
Gran But she wouldn't do that to her mother.
Elsie Given half a chance, I would.
Gran Oh, I don't know though.
Tracy (*sitting at the table*) I'd never do that to you.
Elsie Oh, they're not homes like they used to be. They're marvellous places these days.
Tracy You can still be lonely in them, whether they're marvellous or not.
Elsie She couldn't be any more lonely than being stuck up in that bedroom day in and day out.
Tracy Couldn't we have her back down?
Elsie Don't be silly. There's no room.
Tracy She could sit in that chair. (*Indicating the armchair*)
Elsie If she was down here, she'd *hear* too much and *say* too much and *see* too much, which means she'd *be* too much. I'm better off where she is.
Gran It's not fair to leave me up here all day on my own self.
Tracy Couldn't we have her down on weekends?
Gran I don't even like the bloody wallpaper.
Elsie It took me three weeks to get her to stay in that room. If we have her down now, it'll take me another three to get her back again.
Gran I don't know what she's going to do, come Christmas. She won't let me go down, I know that much. (*Almost to herself*) She'll make them all have dinner up 'ere first.
Elsie Go and wet the tea, will you, Trace?

Tracy exits to the kitchen

Gran I wonder what she's doing. Washing, I suspect. (*She addresses the piggy bank*) What day is it? Thursday? She doesn't wash on a Thursday. Perhaps she's not washing. (*A thought strikes her*) Perhaps it's not Thursday. (*She calls*) Elsie?

There is no reply. Gran persists

Elsie?

Elsie (*going to the hall*) What do you want?
Gran What day is it?
Elsie Thursday.
Gran Tuesday?
Elsie (*losing her temper*) Thursday.
Gran What are you doing? Washing, is it?
Elsie I'm ironing, Mam. You know I do the washing on Mondays.
Gran Where's my cocoa?
Elsie It's coming.
Gran What's that?
Elsie (*impatiently*) I said it's coming.
Gran It's gone quarter to ten.
Elsie (*screaming*) It'll be there now!

Elsie is about to return to the living-room when there is a knock on the door

Gran Somebody at the door.
Elsie (*answering it*) Oh, hello. Come in. Hello Jeffrey.

Mrs Millard and her son Jeffrey enter

Go through.

They do. Elsie is about to follow when Gran calls again

Gran Elsie?
Elsie It's all right, Mam. I've answered it.
Gran Who was it?
Elsie I said it's all right.
Gran Who was there, then?
Elsie I'll send Tracy up with your cocoa when it's ready. (*She goes to the living-room and resumes ironing*)
Gran Who's down there with you, Elsie?

Jeffrey is now sitting in the armchair and Maisie Millard is sitting on a dining chair to the right of the table

Maisie Playing you up, is she?
Elsie Oh, I could scream with her this morning.
Maisie It must be very hard for you.
Elsie (*calling to Tracy in the kitchen*) Make another cup of tea for Mrs Millard will you Trace? (*To Maisie*) What about Jeffrey?
Maisie Yes, he'll have one. Two sugars and no milk.
Elsie (*calling*) And one for Jeffrey. Two sugars and no milk.

At this point Jeffrey produces from a large plastic carrier bag a ball of wool and six or seven inches of knitting. He continues to knit throughout the scene with increasing speed

Maisie Tracy's not in work today then?
Elsie No, she didn't go in this morning.

Maisie and Jeffrey share a knowing look

Maisie There we are then.
Gran Elsie?
Elsie Why isn't Jeffrey in school?
Maisie Oh, he never goes on a Thursday (*to Jeffrey*) do you love?

He shakes his head

No, he's games all morning and PE and science in the afternoon.
Gran (*calling even louder*) Elsie?
Maisie (*glancing towards the ceiling*) Hey, I think your mother's calling you.
Elsie I expect she is. We're late with her cocoa.
Gran I'm sure she doesn't answer me on purpose. (*She calls again*) Who have you got down there with you?
Elsie (*becoming more and more agitated*) She's not giving me any peace to get on with this ironing.
Gran If it's the insurance man, you tell 'im I want to see 'im.
Maisie If you ask me, I think you were better off when she was down here in a chair.
Elsie Oh, I don't know. I can do a little more now that she's in her bedroom.
Gran Elsie?
Maisie Why don't you get one of those intercoms? You know, baby alarms they are.
Elsie You must be joking. if I had one of those things I'd never get her off the other end of it. At least I can pretend I can't hear her now.
Gran (*screaming*) Elsie?
Elsie (*slamming down the iron as she screams*) What?!! (*She heads for the hall in a fury*)
Gran Elsie? (*She keeps calling until Elsie answers*)
Elsie What do you want *now*?
Gran Tell 'im I want to see 'im.
Elsie Who?
Gran The insurance man.
Elsie (*almost in tears*) I haven't seen the bloody insurance man.
Gran All right, all right. There's no need to bloody swear. I thought he was down there with you.
Elsie Are you going to let me get on with this ironing?
Gran Where's my cocoa?
Elsie (*now in a real temper*) Tracy will bring it up when it's ready, now be quiet, will you? (*She storms back into the living-room*)
Maisie Pity you couldn't put her away somewhere.
Elsie No bugger will have her. (*She irons furiously*)
Gran I've forgotten to ask her who's down there now.
Maisie Perhaps she wouldn't be so bad if she didn't get so bored. Why don't you get her a couple of books from the library?
Elsie That's an idea. Perhaps I'll do that.

Tracy enters with a tray of tea

Ah, here we are. (*She sits down*) Take Gran's cocoa up Trace, perhaps we'll have some peace then.

Tracy takes Gran's cocoa and leaves her own cup on the tray. Maisie gives Jeffrey his tea then takes one for herself. She calls to Tracy

Maisie (*laughing*) You'd be better off in work, Trace.

Tracy smiles and exits with the cocoa

(*To Elsie*) She doesn't look well to me.

Elsie She hasn't said she's ill.

Maisie Looking a bit peaky round the gills.

She looks at Jeffrey who nods approvingly

And where's Idris?

Elsie Now, where do you think?

Maisie Up the surgery?

Elsie Well, of course.

Maisie What's wrong with him today?

Elsie He had a funny turn about three o'clock this morning. Thinks it might have been a heart attack.

Maisie (*concerned*) Was it?

Elsie Don't be daft.

Maisie Well, he's forever complaining about his chest.

Elsie Idris is forever complaining!!

Maisie Perhaps he'd feel better if he had a little job.

Elsie Oh, you dare not mention work to Idris. He had a relapse last week at the mere suggestion of it.

Maisie A relapse?

Elsie nods

A relapse of what?

Elsie I don't know. I can't remember. (*Suddenly recalling*) Oh, malaria, I think it was.

Maisie Malaria? Well, I didn't know Idris had been abroad during the war?

Elsie He wasn't. He reckons he caught it in the bloody Home Guard.

Maisie (*standing*) Hey, do you like my new cardigan? (*She shows it off*)

Elsie Oh, it's lovely.

Maisie (*nodding towards Jeffrey*) He finished it yesterday.

Elsie He's done a lovely job on it.

Maisie It only took him three days. He's knitting the buggers faster than I can buy the wool. He reckons he's going to make his father an Aran now, for Christmas, (*to Jeffrey*) aren't you?

Elsie You'd think he'd get fed up with it all the time, wouldn't you?

Maisie Oh, not him. He's not happy unless he's got a pair of knitting needles and a ball of wool in his hands. (*She sits down*)

At this point Tracy enters Gran's bedroom and the attention is immediately focused on that area

Tracy Morning Gran.

Gran 'Ello, lovely.

Tracy I've brought your cocoa.
Gran Thank you. (*She takes it and puts it on the table*) Sit down.

Tracy does

   Who's downstairs?
Tracy Only Mammy and Mrs Millard and Jeffrey.
Gran Who's Jeffrey?
Tracy Her son.
Gran That's that poor little bugger who knits, isn't it?
Tracy (*laughing*) Yes.
Gran She'll have trouble with 'im when he's older, you mark my words.
Tracy He's harmless enough.
Gran I daresay he is. But it's not natural. She shouldn't encourage 'im.
   (*Confidentially*) The trouble there was that when she was carrying 'im, 'er
   'usband wanted a boy and she wanted a girl, and both of them 'ad their
   wish.
Tracy (*laughing*) Oh, Gran, you are funny sometimes.
Gran You listen to what I'm telling you. It's all right for 'er to show off all
   those tea-cosies and scarves 'e can make, but if she's not careful 'e'll grow
   up to be an 'omospectacle, you see if 'e don't. Where's your father? Not
   back from the surgery?
Tracy No.
Gran I don't know 'ow the doctors put up with 'im, indeed I don't.
Tracy Hypochondria is an illness in itself, Gran.
Gran 'Ypochondria? 'E thinks 'e's got enough wrong with 'im now, don't
   tell 'im 'e's got that as well. 'E's 'ad every tablet going, your father. 'E
   showed me the latest lot 'e's on. I swear to God, they're Parma Violets.
   (*She sips her cocoa then puts it back on the table*) And why aren't you in
   work?
Tracy I had a day off today.
Gran Well, hell I can see that.
Tracy I didn't feel well this morning.
Gran What's the matter then?
Tracy I just felt a bit off, that's all.
Gran (*smiling wickedly enquiring*) You 'aven't missed, 'ave you?

Tracy is a little embarrassed and turns slightly away

Tracy Gran!
Gran (*still smiling but now leaning closer*) Well, 'ave you?
Tracy (*almost tempted to confide but deciding not to*) I'll come and fetch
   your cup when you've finished, OK? (*She starts to get up*)
Gran Don't you dare leave me up 'ere all day without answering my
   question. Sit down.
Tracy But I——
Gran Sit down, go on, sit down.

Tracy does so. There is a pause

   Well, are you going to answer me or am I going to 'ave to ask you again?

Tracy (*hesitating, after a pause*) Where's your cards, Gran?
Gran Why?
Tracy Tell my fortune?
Gran (*shaking her head*) No, I don't like doing it for the family.
Tracy Oh, please Gran, for me.
Gran No.
Tracy Oh go on.
Gran No.
Tracy For me, please? (*She takes Gran's arm and kisses her coaxingly on the
  cheek several times*)
Gran (*giving in*) Oh, you spoilt bugger. (*She pecks Tracy on the nose. She
  takes the cards and hands them to Tracy*) There you are, shuffle them and
  cut them into three for Gran.

*As Tracy does this Gran takes from under the pillow a black hat. She puts it
on. This is a ritual she performs every time she tells a fortune*

  You're looking a bit peaky. Still courting that boy from River Row?
Tracy Bobby, yes.
Gran Bobby. There's a name. 'E looks nothing like a policeman to me.
Tracy That's not why they call him Bobby.
Gran Does 'e still wear that old earring?
Tracy Yes.
Gran I'll never forget the day you brought 'im up 'ere to see me. (*Pointing to
  the floor*) There 'e stood with 'is long 'air—'as 'e 'ad it cut?

Tracy nods

  'E was wearing a shirt not unlike the blouse I got married in. And by the
  state of it, it could 'ave been the same one.
Tracy They're all the fashion.
Gran There 'e was, anyway. I tell you, 'e frightened me. If I 'adn't seen you
  standing next to 'im I'd 'ave thought 'e was an old gypsy come to sell me
  pegs.
Tracy (*laughing*) Come to sell you pegs?
Gran Ay. And I'll tell you, Tracy, 'e frightened me so much, if 'e 'ad been
  selling pegs, I'd 'ave bought the buggers.
Tracy (*displaying the cards on the bed*) There you are. Is that right?
Gran You're sure you want this done?
Tracy Yes.
Gran Right then. (*She takes one set of cards and begins to study them*)

The action is taken up downstairs

Maisie ... well, of course he will, (*to Jeffrey*) won't you?

Jeffrey nods

  He knitted our Carol a beautiful two-piece suit. Green it was, and it had a
  lovely line to it. But do you know, it took fifty-three and a half ounces.
Elsie (*incredulously*) That's a lot of balls!
Maisie No, it did, honest.

The action returns upstairs

Gran (*still looking at the cards*) I can see a man 'ere with a bald 'ead. Suffers with alopecia.

Tracy It's not Dad, is it?

Gran Don't tell 'im 'e's going bald, for God's sake, or 'is 'air *will* fall out. Anyway, do you know 'im?

Tracy Bobby's father's bald.

Gran Is he indeed? Well, you want to be careful there then.

Tracy What do you mean?

Gran Well, like father like son. If Noddy's father is going bald, the chances are that 'e will too. It's like that, baldness. It's chiropody.

Tracy You mean hereditary.

Gran Don't contracept me.

Tracy (*correcting her*) Contradict.

Gran There you go again. I 'ope you don't do that to your Nobby, do you? 'Cause a man don't like to be contracepted by a woman all the time. Now, is this man your financie's father or not?

Tracy It sounds like him.

Gran Well, whoever 'e is, 'e's dressed up to the nines. 'E's got a suit on.

Tracy What colour?

Gran (*pointing to the cards*) Grey. A big grey check. (*Making a face as she turns her head away from the cards*) Ugh, it's so big it's giving me a 'eadache looking at it.

Tracy That's Bobby's father, I'm sure.

Gran 'E's wearing a flower in his lapel. A carnation. (*Facing Tracy*) Not going to a wedding, is 'e?

Tracy (*swallowing hard*) I don't know.

Gran Funny, I can't see a lady with 'im.

Tracy He's a widower.

Gran Well, with a suit like that, I'm not surprised. (*She cackles*)

The action moves back downstairs

Maisie ... of course, I've sworn not to tell you, but I may as well, because find out you will, I expect. (*A little more confidentially*) I didn't want to say anything because it's about your Tracy—and that boy.

At this point Jeffrey stops knitting and leans slightly to his left as he tunes into the conversation

Elsie (*indignant*) What's it got to do with them?

Maisie Oh, nothing. Nothing, I'm sure. It's just that ... well ... (*she moves her chair closer to Elsie*) ... there's a rumour going around that one of those boys, and there's only two isn't there, Bobby and his brother, well one of those boys has got some little girl into trouble—and I didn't want to say anything in case it was your Tracy and she hadn't said anything. (*She pauses then enquires tentatively*) She hasn't said anything?

Elsie (*astounded at the nerve of the woman*) No!!

Maisie No, must be the other boy then. I thought it was, to be honest with you. I couldn't see Tracy doing something silly like that. (*Again she tentatively enquires*) Could you?

Elsie (*booming her reply*) No!!

Jeffrey immediately resumes his knitting at breakneck speed

Maisie (*shaking her head*) No. *Must* be the other one then. (*After a slight pause*) Pity, in a way——

Elsie looks at her furiously

—if you know what I mean, because when I was telling Jeffrey about it, he said if it was Tracy, *if* it was her, he would have been quite prepared to have made a couple of pairs of bootees and a matinée coat. (*To Jeffrey*) Wouldn't you?

The action returns upstairs

Gran (*still looking at the cards*) Well, you may was well know it Tracy, I don't like what I see.

Tracy What can you see?

Gran Not much, pass my glasses.

Tracy opens Gran's handbag and takes out the glasses

Ta, love. (*She puts them on*) That's better. (*She looks at the cards again*) I still don't like it though. You're upset, aren't you?

Tracy (*trying to cover up*) No.

Gran Yes, you are, aren't you?

Tracy (*trying to laugh*) No.

Gran (*insisting*) Yes you are, you're upset.

Tracy I'm not.

Gran Well, you should be.

Tracy Why?

Gran (*indicating the cards*) Because it says so here, that's why.

Tracy (*pausing, then speaking rather excitedly*) I think I'm in love, Gran.

Gran (*shocked*) In love? With who? Not that old gypsy?

Tracy (*laughing*) He's not a gypsy.

Gran Go on. You don't know anything about love.

Tracy Yes, I do.

Gran (*smiling to herself*) It's not just sex, you know that, don't you?

Tracy Yes. It's looking after him, as well.

Gran Love isn't washing 'is dirty socks, Tracy. Love is that special feeling you get inside *when* you wash them. (*She sighs then looks at the cards again*) You do love 'im though, 'cause I can see it in the cards.

Tracy What about him, Gran?

Gran What about 'im?

Tracy Does *he* love *me*?

Gran Well, you shouldn't need me to tell you that.

Tracy I want to know if it's in the cards.

Gran Let's 'ave a look, then. (*She looks at the cards again*) I can see a lot of tears Tracy. Not all of them are sad though. Some of them are tears of joy. You are going to be very 'appy. But I can see a big grey cloud 'ere, lots of tears. You're going to lose somebody, Tracy.

They look at each other

Somebody close to you.

Tracy starts to interrupt

Now I'm not saying it's your Nobby, but there's going to be a loss. A death in the family.

Tracy (*after a slight pause*) Oh, Gran.

There is a loud clap of thunder and several flashes of lightning. Tracy and Gran look up to the skylight

The action moves downstairs

Maisie ... Well, why don't you go and see about it?

Elsie I'll have to. I'm gone, I'm in agony.

Maisie I expect you are.

Elsie I don't like bothering the doctors though. God knows, they've got enough to put up with with our Idris.

At this point Jeffrey pulls his mother to her feet. She is still facing Elsie and Jeffrey measures his knitting against her back. Then they both return to their chairs

Maisie You're going to have to have it seen to in case it turns into something serious. Lots of illnesses are caused by neglect.

Elsie To be honest, I'm afraid to see about it. Afraid of what they might find.

Maisie Oh, it's nothing to worry about. And the sooner you have it looked at, the better. (*A slight pause*) Hey, I'll have a look at it for you if you like.

Elsie (*very quickly*) No, no. It's all right thank you.

Maisie Have you told Idris yet?

Elsie I haven't told anyone. Well, only you.

Maisie Oh, you don't have to worry about me. I won't say anything.

She and Jeffrey share a look

I do think you should tell Idris though.

Elsie There's no point. He'll only swear he's got it as well.

Maisie But it's a woman's complaint.

Elsie That won't make any difference to Idris.

The action returns upstairs

Gran I'm looking at a 'ospital 'ere. I can't see who's in bed, but everybody is laughing and joking so it can't be anything serious. (*She begins to laugh hysterically*)

Tracy (*starting to laugh with her*) What's the matter?

Gran is laughing too much to answer

Why are you laughing?

Gran (*still hysterical*) It's that man with a check suit.
Tracy Bobby's father?
Gran (*laughing louder than ever*) 'E's 'ere again. (*She stops laughing abruptly*) 'Aven't he got another suit? (*She laughs again*)
Tracy Why are you laughing, Gran?
Gran E's not wearing a flower this time.
Tracy Tell me Gran.
Gran Tell you what, my lovely? (*Still laughing*)
Tracy Why are you laughing?

Gran thinks for a moment then expresses slight confusion

Gran 'Ell, I've forgotten now.

The action moves downstairs

Maisie Well, thanks for the tea. I think we'd better make a move.

She stands. Jeffrey looks at her sharply, rather annoyed

Oh, all right, go on, finish the row. (*To Elsie*) He doesn't like stopping in the middle. Did it once, dropped a stitch—three-quarters of an hour to pick it back up (*She sits*)

The action returns upstairs

Gran Who's Deborah?
Tracy I don't know.
Gran Well, she's in your cards, anyway. Remember the name—Deborah. (*She looks at the cards, then at Tracy, suspiciously*) I can see a bird, too.
Tracy A bird?
Gran Ay. A big bugger. With a long neck and legs to match.
Tracy (*physically stiffening*) A turkey?
Gran No.
Gran (*frantically thinking of another bird*) A peacock?
Gran No.
Tracy (*now really worried*) A pelican?
Gran No.

They look at each other

A stork!

Tracy realizes she has been found out

The action moves downstairs

Maisie (*standing up*) Right then, I'll see you.

Elsie immediately makes for the front door

I don't want to stop you getting on with your work. I know how busy you are with all that ironing, (*to Jeffrey*) and we've got to go and get something for Daddy's——(*she sees Elsie and realizes she has out-stayed her welcome*)—come on Jeffrey. (*To Elsie*) Don't forget what I said and get her (*she points to the ceiling*) a couple of books. She'll be right for you then.

Elsie Yes, perhaps I'll do that.

Maisie And go and have someone to have a look at your ... (*She mouths something unidentifiable*)

Elsie Yes, I will. (*She shows them out*)

Maisie and Jeffrey go out the front door

Maisie (*off*) Say so-long, Jeffrey.

He doesn't

Elsie Oh it's going to rain, I think. It's come over all dark. See you. Ta-rah. (*She starts to go back to the living-room then turns back to the bottom of the stairs and shouts*) Tracy?

Tracy What?

Elsie You've let your tea go cold.

Tracy All right, I'll be down now.

Elsie goes back to the living-room and resumes her ironing

Action upstairs

Gran Well, I don't know what your mother and father are going to say.

Tracy I don't know how to tell them.

Gran It's not your place to tell 'em. 'E should do it, that Noddy, not you. (*She smiles wickedly*) Your grandfather did.

A slight pause, then Tracy realizes what Gran has said. They both laugh

Oh, you're not the first and neither was I. Now, you tell your Roddy——

Tracy Bobby.

Gran Bobby, yes. You tell 'im to come 'ere and tell 'em tonight.

Tracy (*a little uneasy*) Oh, he can't tell them tonight, Gran.

Gran Why not?

Tracy Because he doesn't know himself yet.

Gran (*sympathetically*) Will 'e marry you?

Tracy I don't know. I think so.

Gran Oh, it's 'orrible being a woman. It's not fair. If you say no, they think you're a lesbeen, if you say yes, they think you're loose. (*Smiling wickedly*) They coax you for months—and when you finally give in they leave you standing. Or as in my case—'anging!

Tracy (*shocked*) Hanging?!!

Gran Yes. But I won't go into that now.

Tracy He said he'd marry me if anything went wrong.

Gran They all say that, love. Your grandfather bribed me with a weekend trip to London, shopping.

Tracy Did you enjoy it?

Gran I never bloody went. By the time 'e'd saved up enough money. I was 'aving your mother.

Tracy I didn't know you had to get married, Gran.

Gran (*smiling again*) Yes, well you didn't know your grandfather, did you?
Tracy (*also smiling*) Wouldn't leave you alone, would he?
Gran (*becoming excited*) Well, I don't know how to put this—but *no* 'E 'ad a very big appetite, your grandfather. 'E wasn't 'appy with the meat and potatoes like everyone else. 'E 'ad to 'ave the soup and the apple tart as well. Do you know what I mean?
Tracy (*taken up with Gran's enthusiasm*) Yes.
Gran (*shouting*) Well, you shouldn't. No wonder you're in bloody trouble.
Tracy It happened to you too.
Gran *I* was *twenty-nine!*
Tracy That seems even worse, somehow.
Gran What did your Roddy promise you, apart from marriage?
Tracy Nothing.
Gran Nothing? Oh well, there you are then; not going to be disappointed, are you?
Tracy I didn't want him to bribe me with anything. Anyway, I've been to London twice.
Gran (*showing Tracy the cards*) Do you want me to go on with these?
Tracy No, I'd better go down.
Gran Come up and see me after then, will you?
Tracy Yes all right.
Gran This afternoon.
Tracy (*standing up*) Is there anything you want. Say now, Gran, before I go down.
Gran No nothing.
Tracy Are you sure?
Gran Nothing. I don't want nothing. My eyes are burning, I'm going to 'ave a little five minutes. (*She closes her eyes and settles down*)

Tracy leaves the bedroom and seconds later she enters the hall and goes into the living-room

Tracy They've gone then?
Elsie Yes. (*After a slight pause*) You were upstairs a long time.
Tracy (*sitting on a chair next to the table*) I was talking to Gran. (*After a slight hesitation*) She told my fortune when I was up there.
Elsie I thought she didn't like doing it for the family.
Tracy I coaxed her. She told me there was going to be a death in the family.
Elsie Well, you don't want to say too much about that, do you? It'll be fatal if it fell on the wrong ears. (*Looking at Tracy*) You know what I mean.
Tracy Perhaps it's Auntie Dot.
Elsie She's only gone in to have her sinuses done. (*After a slight pause*) What else did she tell you?
Tracy (*biting her lip*) She told me I was upset.
Elsie (*glancing at her*) Are you?
Tracy Well, I am a bit.
Elsie What has a young girl like you to be upset about?
Tracy I'm pregnant.
Elsie You've got everything going for you. You've got a nice face, nice

clothes, nice—pregnant?!! (*She slams down the iron and begins to cry*) Pregnant?

Tracy (*standing*) Oh, now don't get upset, Mam.

Elsie What's your father going to say?

Tracy Come and sit down. (*She guides Elsie to the settee*)

At this point, the front door opens and Idris enters, slamming the door behind him

Gran is the only one who hears this and sits bolt upright in bed

Gran Somebody at the door!

Tracy It'll be all right, Mam, I'm only eight weeks.

Elsie Eight weeks? (*She cries even louder*)

Gran Who's there?

Idris takes off his scarf and overcoat and hangs them in the hall. He then tunes in to the conversation in the living-room and assumes that Elsie and Tracy are talking about him

Elsie Oh, I never thought something like this would happen.

Tracy (*trying to comfort her*) Come on, Mam, it's not the end of the world.

Elsie (*screaming*) It will be for your father.

Idris takes one step nearer to the living-room

Gran Elsie?

Elsie Who's going to tell him?

Tracy I thought you would.

Elsie (*hysterical*) Oh, no. I can't do it. I shouldn't be the one.

Tracy Bobby'll have to then.

Idris half-turns to the front of the stage and mimes "Bobby"

Gran What's going on down there?

Elsie (*trying to pull herself together*) Perhaps we shouldn't say anything for a while. You know what he's like.

Idris has now turned to face the living-room again

Tracy I think he should be told now.

Elsie (*hysterical again*) But he won't be able to take it.

Idris puts his hand to his throat and rushes to the hall mirror where he immediately sticks out his tongue

Tracy Well, he'll have to.

Elsie We haven't got much time have we? How long did you say?

Tracy Eight weeks.

Elsie Eight weeks.

Idris faces front and mimes "Eight weeks"

(*A little calmer but still upset*) We'll have to start making plans, preparations. I've got an endowment coming out soon. (*Crying again*) Oh I never thought something like this would happen.

Idris begins to stagger in the hall. He checks his pulse, taps his chest "doctor-like", feels for a pulse in his neck, then puts his hand between his legs and coughs

Tracy (*sitting next to Elsie on the settee*) Oh, don't worry.

Elsie (*screaming*) I don't know how you can be so calm. It's going to put an end to your father! It's going to put an end to him!

Idris collapses in the hall. We hear a loud thunderclap

Black-out

CURTAIN

ACT II

The same. Evening of the same day

As the scene opens, Gran is sitting upright in bed with her eyes closed. She is semi-conscious. Idris is lounging on the settee and has a crêpe bandage around his head

After a few seconds Tracy pops her head around the kitchen door

Tracy I'm making tea, Dad. Do you want a cup?
Idris (*weakly*) No, not for me.

Tracy disappears

I'll have a glass of Lucozade though.
Tracy (*off*) All right.
Idris Bring my tablets in while you're out there, will you Tracy?
Tracy (*off*) Which ones?
Idris (*looking at his watch*) My half-past seven ones.
Tracy Are they green or black?
Idris (*raising his voice a little*) Blue. Two blue ones. (*After a pause*) I didn't think your mother would have gone out tonight. Not after I had my funny turn.
Tracy (*off*) She promised Auntie Dot.
Idris I shouldn't be left.

Tracy enters from the kitchen

Tracy You're not left. I'm here—and Bobby's coming round.
Idris (*physically stiffening*) What's he coming here for?
Tracy (*awkwardly*) Well ... to see you.
Idris (*frightened*) What does he want to see me for?
Tracy We're staying in tonight, that's all. So he's coming round.
Idris I hope he's got rid of that flu. He was full of it the last time he was here.
Tracy Only *I* caught it.
Idris *I* sneezed for three days.
Tracy I'll get your Lucozade.

She exits to the kitchen

Idris (*calling after her*) I don't want it hot, mind.

There is a knock on the front door. Gran immediately awakens

Gran Somebody at the door! (*She leans forward to listen*)

Idris (*calling*) Tracy, there's somebody at the door.
Tracy (*off*) Well, answer it, then.
Gran (*calling*) There's somebody at the door.
Idris But what about my back?
Tracy You won't break it answering the door.
Idris I'm not supposed to exert myself.

There is another knock on the door

Gran Idris?
Idris Tracy?
Tracy (*off; losing her temper*) Answer it then, I'm pouring the tea.
Idris (*rising and going to the door*) You've got no consideration for the sick, Tracy, that's what's the matter with you.
Gran (*calling*) Tracy. Idris. Will somebody answer that door.
Idris (*opening the door*) Oh, hello. Come in.

Bobby enters and stands in the hallway. He is wearing leather boots, jeans, leather jacket and crash helmet

Go through.
Gran Where is everybody?

Idris and Bobby enter the living-room

Idris Sit down.

Bobby is about to sit in Idris' place on the settee. Idris clears his throat abruptly and Bobby jumps back up before his bottom has touched the settee

Sit over there, look (*He points to the armchair*)

Bobby goes

Tracy's in the kitchen. (*Calling to Tracy*) Tracy, it's for you ... it's Rodney.
Bobby (*correcting him*) Er ... Bobby. (*He takes off his helmet to reveal punk-style multi-coloured hair*)
Gran I bet they've left me in this 'ouse all on my own self.
Idris We're just going to have a cup of tea; fancy a cup?
Bobby Er ... no fank you, Mr Roberts.
Idris Tracy's making it, mind.
Bobby (*after a slight pause*) Oh. Better 'ad then.
Idris (*calling*) Make an extra cup for Bobby, Tracy.
Gran They shouldn't do that. It's wrong.
Idris You got rid of that flu then?

Bobby is looking in another direction and after a few seconds realizes that Idris might have been addressing him. He looks at him questioningly

That flu. You were full of it the last time you were here.
Bobby (*remembering*) Oh, yeah. I'm better now, fank you Mr Roberts.

Pause. Bobby looks away but becomes aware of Idris staring at him. He looks over at him again

Yeah, I'm better now.

They look at each other. Idris nods encouragingly at Bobby. Bobby feels that something is expected of him but he doesn't know what. He looks away again. Idris gives up and mutters under his breath. In order to break the silence Bobby asks Idris casually . . .

How are you feeling Mr——

Idris (*pouncing on his question before he finishes*) It's funny you should ask, Bobby. I'm not a healthy man, as you know but . . . well, things haven't been too good for me lately, you know. I had a funny turn earlier. I collapsed out in the hall. I was there for over an hour before they found me.

Bobby Anyfing serious?

Idris (*enthusiastically*) Oh, I expect so. It's not like me to have anything trivial. I went to visit a friend of mine in hospital once, you know. Visiting was only from seven 'til eight. I ended up staying three days.

Bobby Taken bad were you?

Idris No. I hit my head on the "Mind your Head" sign. Do you know, I had to have twenty-one stiches.

Bobby (*incredulously*) In your 'ead?

Idris No. In my trousers. As I fell I split open one of the seams.

Bobby Well, you seem to be looking all right now Mr Roberts. You got a smashing colour.

Idris Don't let that fool you. (*Touching his cheek*) Don't mistake this rosy-cheeked complexion for health. That's my blood-pressure, that is.

Bobby I didn't know you 'ad that, as well.

Idris People don't know half, Bobby, they don't know half. The tragic thing is, of course, I can't keep a job like most people. I keep catching different things. You can keep your money and the rest. Give me a clean bill of health every time. It's these hypochondriacs I don't have time for. Do you know, I go to the out-patients three or four times a week and I see the same faces. They're all there, all of them. All lined up with everything wrong with them from A to Z. It's not fair. Doctors and nurses have a hard enough time of it without having to put up with people like that.

Tracy enters carrying a small tray. On it are two cups of tea, a cup of cocoa and a glass of Lucozade and two tablets. She smiles at Bobby then goes to Idris

Tracy Take this cup of cocoa up to Gran, will you Dad?

Idris Now you know I get trouble with the stairs.

Tracy (*winking at Bobby*) If you don't exercise your arthritis, it'll get better, mind.

Idris thinks it over for a minute then points to Gran's cup

Idris That one's hers, is it? (*He picks it up*) I'll have mine when I come back down.

He exits to the hallway, checking himself in the hall mirror as he passes, then goes upstairs

Tracy (*sitting on the settee*) Come and sit over here.
Bobby (*sitting next to her*) I fought p'raps we'd go to ver pictures tonight, Trace?
Tracy I think we'd better stay in and save the money.
Bobby (*disappointed*) Aw, but I 'aven't seen *Pinocchio*.
Tracy (*coaxingly*) Let's have a nice night in instead, is it?
Bobby (*relenting*) OK. If you want to. (*He sips his tea*)
Tracy (*after a pause*) Tea all right?
Bobby Yeah, lovely.
Tracy I make a nice cup of tea, don't I?
Bobby (*nodding*) Yeah, nice.
Tracy My mother's going to teach me how to boil eggs tomorrow.
Bobby That's nice.
Tracy You like them in sandwiches, don't you?
Bobby Yeah, lovely.
Tracy (*after a pause*) Hey, Debbie Thomas got engaged last week.
Bobby That's nice.
Tracy (*annoyed*) Can't you say anything else?
Bobby Course I can. (*He looks at her and smiles*) You make a lovely cup of tea.

The action moves upstairs

Gran (*frightened*) Who's there? Who's there? Come on, I know you are there. (*She takes a huge wooden mallet from under the bedclothes*) You're not a burglar, are you? All my money's in the Post Office and I've got nothing else you want, I'm eighty-one. Come on, let's be 'aving——

Idris enters with the cocoa

Oh, Idris, you frightened me, you simple-looking bugger. I thought we 'ad burglars and I was on my own self in this 'ouse. (*She puts the mallet back under the sheets*)
Idris I've brought you a cup of cocoa.
Gran Oh, thank you. (*She takes it from him and puts it on the bedside table*) Who's downstairs?
Idris Only Tracy and her boyfriend.
Gran It was 'im at the door, was it?

He nods

I knew I 'eard somebody. I shout for 'ours up 'ere and nobody takes any notice. (*Pointing to the chairs*) Sit down, Idris.
Idris (*agitated*) No, I'm not stopping.
Gran I want to tell your fortune.
Idris (*backing away*) I don't want it done.
Gran Sit down.
Idris But I——
Gran (*scornfully*) Idris. (*She takes her hat from under the bedclothes and puts it on*)

Idris knows it's pointless protesting and sits down

You're not afraid are you?
Idris I don't want to hear anything bad.
Gran I'll only tell you what I see; I can't tell you anything else.
Idris Half of it is rubbish, anyway.
Gran (*taking a pack of cards from under her pillow*) Shuffle and cut the cards. (*She hands them to him*)
Idris (*as he shuffles them*) Tell me now then.
Gran What, boy?
Idris What if there's nothing there? I mean, what if you can't see anything?
Gran You'll be dead by the morning.

Idris releases the cards and he and Gran are showered by them. Gran cackles. During the following scene Idris collects the cards and cuts them into three

The action moves downstairs

Tracy Bobby?
Bobby Yeah?
Tracy Do you love me?
Bobby (*after a slight pause*) Yeah.
Tracy Tell me then.
Bobby What for?
Tracy So that I'll know.
Bobby You already know.
Tracy But you haven't told me.
Bobby (*embarrassed*) I can't.
Tracy Why?
Bobby I don't know what to say.
Tracy Just say "I love you".
Bobby (*after thinking it over for a moment*) No I can't. It's daft.
Tracy No it's not. You do love me, don't you?
Bobby Yeah.
Tracy Well, say it then.
Bobby (*forcing himself*) I lo ... I lo ... I ... I wish we'd gone to ver pictures.

Action upstairs

Gran (*looking at one set of cards*) It's all right Idris, don't worry, I think you'll see the night through. (*She pauses for a moment*) Who do you know that wears a surgical collar?
Idris No-one. (*He feels his neck*)
Gran Well, somebody's going to 'ave one within a four. (*Looking at Idris*) No prizes for guessing who! You're thinking about going away for a 'oliday.
Idris (*amazed that she has hit on something true*) Yes.
Gran Well don't.
Idris (*frightened*) Why? 'Cause I won't be here?

Gran No, 'cause I won't let you. I'm not staying in this 'ouse on my own self. (*Looking at the cards again*) You're thinking about buying a new suit.
Idris No, I'm not.
Gran Well, somebody's thinking about buying you one. Our Elsie I expect. (*Shaking her head*) Tell her not to bother. Tell 'er to 'ave your old one cleaned.
Idris (*really frightened*) Oh, my God.
Gran I can see a big building too. A church or chapel or something. I can't quite make it out.
Idris (*becoming upset*) And cars?
Gran Oh, yes. Lots of cars.
Idris (*fighting back tears*) Black ones?
Gran Yes, two or three black ones. And flowers. Look Idris.

She shows him the cards but he turns away

Look. I don't think I've ever seen so many beautiful flowers.
Idris (*almost uncontrollable*) And I'm not there am I?
Gran Yes, Idris, you are there.
Idris (*relieved*) Oh, thank God for that.
Gran You're in the big black car in the front.

Gran cackles as Idris almost collapses

Action downstairs

Tracy Bobby?
Bobby Yeah?
Tracy Do you remember your twenty-first birthday party?
Bobby Yeah.
Tracy (*suggestively*) Do you remember what I gave you?
Bobby (*smiling knowingly*) Yeah.
Tracy Do you remember saying that if anything went wrong ...
Bobby Yeah.
Tracy (*after a slight pause*) Well, it went wrong.
Bobby (*after pausing*) Oh!
Idris (*frantically*) I don't want to hear any more, I've heard enough. (*He rises and moves slightly forward*)
Tracy Is that all you're going to say.
Gran But I 'aven't finished yet.
Bobby Are you sure?
Tracy Positive.
Idris I know I've only got so long.
Gran Somebody's going to give you some news.
Tracy Did you mean what you said?
Idris Oh, yes, and I know exactly who it is.
Tracy You didn't tell me that just to have your own way?
Idris It's him downstairs.
Tracy Bobby?
Bobby Yeah?

Tracy Say something.
Gran You're going to be surprised.
Bobby What are we going to do?
Tracy What are *we* going to do?
Idris I heard them planning it all this morning. That's why he's come round.
Gran You mustn't take it too 'ard.
Tracy You'll have to tell my father.
Bobby Yeah.
Tracy Tonight.
Bobby Yeah.
Gran It comes to us all.
Idris But I'm too young.
Bobby Oh, no I can't. Not tonight.
Tracy You'll have to, it's not my place.
Bobby But what will I say?
Gran You can't get out of it.
Tracy You can't get out of it, Bobby.
Gran When the news comes you must take it like a man.
Idris (*trying desperately to control himself*) Yes.
Gran It's not going to be easy.
Idris No.
Gran So be understanding.
Idris That's right.
Gran It's going to be difficult enough for the one who 'as to tell you.
Idris I know.
Gran So you 'elp 'im as much as you can.
Idris Yes.
Gran Are you satisfied?
Idris Yes.
Gran Good. That'll be fifty p. (*She holds out her hand*)

Idris digs out fifty pence and gives it to her

Idris I'd best go down, then.
Gran Aye, aye.
Idris It could happen to anyone, see.
Gran Aye.
Idris Just so happened that it happened to me, that's all.
Gran Aye.

Idris leaves the room

Poor bugger. (*She cackles as she drops the money into her piggy bank*)

Action downstairs

Tracy Just start off by telling him what you think of me. (*She thinks about what she has said*) No ... no, no second thoughts ...
Bobby I want to marry you Trace, but I just can't bring myself to tell your father.

Tracy It'll be all right, don't worry. He's not a monster. If he tries being difficult just breathe on him, he bruises easily.

At this point Idris enters the hall. He is about to enter the living-room when he overhears the following

Bobby I won't be able to find the words, I know I won't.
Tracy Stop worrying.
Bobby If I dry up you'll help me out, won't you?
Tracy Oh, I can't. I won't be here. I'm going upstairs to sit with Gran.
Bobby Don't leave me on my own Trace, I'll never be able to tell——

Bobby looks up and sees Idris standing there. He and Tracy both get up quickly, feeling very awkward

Tracy Oh, Dad, you're back down. (*After a slight pause*) Gran all right?
Idris (*swallowing hard*) Yes.
Tracy I think I'll go up and see her. (*To Bobby*) I'll see you later. (*She starts to leave the room and when she passes Idris, she turns round to gesture to Bobby*)

Idris almost catches her

She hurries upstairs

During the next scene, Tracy enters Gran's bedroom to find her asleep. She sits at the bedside with Gran's hand in hers, stroking Gran's hair

Idris and Bobby look at each other for a minute. Idris takes one small step into the room and Bobby simultaneously takes one small step backwards. Still staring at each other they repeat this twice more

Idris (*nervously*) Sit down.
Bobby (*equally nervously*) No fank you, Mr Roberts.
Idris Drink?
Bobby No fank you, Mr Roberts.
Idris Whisky or gin?
Bobby (*without hesitation*) Gin.

Idris attends to the drinks

I shouldn't drink it really, 'cause it always makes me cry.
Idris That's funny. It always makes me feel like that, as well.

There is an embarrassed pause

Bobby Been a lovely day, Mr Roberts.
Idris I hope you like them big, do you?
Bobby (*misunderstanding*) Pardon?
Idris The gins.
Bobby Oh, yeah.

He laughs as Idris hands him one

Lovely. (*He takes a sip and then gasps at the strength of it*)

Idris Too much tonic?
Bobby (*hardly able to speak*) No, that's lovely, fank you, Mr Roberts.
Idris Cheers. (*He drinks*)
Bobby To your good health.

Idris almost chokes

Yes, they are a bit strong, aren't they?

There is a pause. They look at each other, both waiting for the other one to begin. Eventually Bobby starts

I've ... I've got somefing to tell you Mr Roberts ...

Not quite ready to hear the inevitable Idris retreats physically and verbally by telling his own story

Idris I remember when I was a little boy, Bobby, I was taken bad with rheumatic fever——
Bobby (*having made his approach he decides to carry it through*) But I don't know how to start——
Idris I didn't want to tell my mother, of course, because I didn't want her to worry——
Bobby I don't want to upset you——
Idris —but you can't keep something like that to yourself——(*He sits on the settee*)
Bobby —because everyfing will be all right——
Idris —so when there's something wrong, it's best to come out in the open with it.
Bobby I can promise you that.
Idris I'll be very understanding.
Bobby Will you?
Idris (*after a slight pause*) Pardon?
Bobby Be very understanding?
Idris (*almost afraid to ask*) About what?
Bobby About what I 'ave to tell you.

Suddenly Idris rises to his feet. As he does so Bobby sits down in the armchair, creating a see-saw effect Idris pulls himself together and speaks with all the inner strength he can muster

Idris I was never permitted to fight for my country Bobby. Never had the opportunity to show how brave and courageous I can be, you see, because I had a pierced ear.
Bobby (*feeling his earlobe*) Oh, I've got one of vose.
Idris (*a little impatient at being misunderstood*) The correct term for the condition is a perforated eardrum. Anyway, God has seen fit, now that I have reached this "delicate" age, to bring forth a situation in which I can prove my strength and courage. (*He begins to lose control of his emotions*) And like the men who met their end in the trenches, (*quite emotional now*) I'll meet mine here, (*tears are flowing*) in my little castle—with my family. (*He slumps down on the settee*)

Not knowing how to proceed with the conversation, Bobby knocks back the last of his drink

Action upstairs

    Tracy has been sitting at the bedside with Gran's hand in hers, stroking Gran's hair. Suddenly Gran awakes

Gran Who's that?

Tracy It's all right Gran, it's only me.

Gran I must 'ave dropped off. I thought you wouldn't be long.

Tracy I've left Bobby down with Dad for a bit.

Gran I don't think you've got anything to worry about. I've paved the way for you.

Tracy What do you mean?

Gran Well, when your father came up 'ere with my cocoa, I told 'is fortune. Or at least he thinks I did. I told 'im I could see a church, chapel, cars, flowers—(*she cackles*)—I think he got the message.

Tracy You didn't tell him anything else, did you?

Gran No, why?

Tracy Well, he looked a bit strange when he came back down.

Gran I know he's your father, Tracy, but he's always looked a bit strange to me. I broke my 'eart when your mother said she was bringing a man 'ome and walked in with 'im.

Tracy (*laughing*) Go on, Gran.

Gran We 'ad a dog in them days too. Sheba. I'll never forget it. She took one look at your father, darted out of the front door and threw 'erself under a bus. I cried for a month.

Tracy Because of the dog?

Gran Yes. But you shouldn't call names like that on your father. (*She cackles*)

Action downstairs

Idris Life's a funny thing, Bobby.

Bobby looks at him

    I don't mean funny ...

He laughs and so does Bobby

    I mean funny ...

He cries and so does Bobby

    No, no. (*Pulling himself together*) I'm not going to get upset. I'm going to face this situation like a man. I'll tell you what, (*he rises and takes Bobby's glass*) let's have another drink.

Bobby Fank you. (*After a pause*) About Tracy——

Idris I knew it was only a matter of time, of course.

Bobby (*surprised*) Did you?

Idris Oh yes. (*Pouring drinks at the sideboard*) Well, life's like that, isn't it?

You are born and you die. We all have to do things we don't want to do. I
suppose we could make it easier for ourselves. (*He moves to Bobby with
the drinks*) I mean—you don't want to tell me what it is you have to tell
me and personally, personally Bobby, I don't want to hear it. That
doesn't make it go away, of course. (*He hands Bobby his drink*) But I think
it would be better all round if we consider the matter said and leave it at
that.

Bobby (*delighted*) Oh, fank you very much, Mr Roberts.

Idris (*moving to the settee*) It doesn't make my situation any easier, mind
you.

Bobby I do everyfing I can to help.

Idris (*sitting on the settee*) You're a good one Bobby. (*Starting to get upset*)

Bobby (*also getting upset*) I'll look after Tracy, I promise you that.

Idris (*giving way to his emotion*) I knew you would.

Bobby (*crying*) Cheers.

Idris (*also crying*) Cheers, boy.

*As Bobby and Idris are crying, the action is taken upstairs with Tracy and
Gran laughing*

Tracy I bet when Daddy finds out he's going to be a grandad, he'll be
laughing all over his face.

Gran I wouldn't like to say what 'is reaction will be.

Tracy Well, he's bound to be pleased, after the initial shock, don't you
think?

Gran (*shaking her head*) When your mother told 'im he was going to be a
father, he didn't speak to anyone for three days.

Tracy Why's that?

Gran He fell into a coma. *He* carried you, of course, you know that don't
you? Or so he'd 'ave you believe.

At this point Idris is relating the same story to Bobby but in mime

He went through all the motions from morning sickness to toxaemia. Yes,
you and your mother 'ad a wonderful birth, but he only just pulled
through. The doctors advised your mother not to 'ave any more children,
on account of your father's 'eart.

Tracy What's the matter with his heart, then?

Gran Don't tell me you don't know?

Tracy No.

Gran He reckons it's not 'is.

Tracy Well, if it's not his, whose is it?

Gran 'Is brother's.

Tracy He hasn't got a brother.

Gran I know. You're not grasping this at all, are you love?

Tracy shakes her head

No. Well, if you listen to your father, he reckons that when 'is mother and
father, you know when he was received——

Tracy (*correcting her*) Conceived.

Gran That's right. When he was received, he was twins. Then 'is mother fell getting out of a coal lorry and somehow

She claps her hands and Idris does the same simultaneously

—the two mingled together. And that's 'ow he says he's got a split personality.

Tracy He hasn't got a split personality.

Gran Oh, yes he 'ave. He's under a psychiatrist anyway. And so he should be, going round telling people he's got 'is brother's 'eart.

Tracy Well, if he thinks he's got his brother's heart, what happened to his own?

Gran Oh, he reckons he's got that was well. I tell you Tracy, your father is a walking miracle.

Action downstairs

Idris The truth of the matter is, see Bobby, I'm a walking miracle.

Bobby I fink you must be, Mr Roberts.

Idris It's a miracle I was ever born at all, you know.

Bobby Is that right?

Idris Oh, yes. Well according to my father anyway. He worked nights for twenty years.

Bobby I still find it 'ard to believe that you 'ad four massive coronaries. Last night.

Idris (*nodding as he puts his hand on his chest*) Yes. My doctor says I'm a very lucky man.

There is a knock at the door

Gran Somebody at the door.

Bobby I fink vere's somebody at the door, Mr Roberts.

Idris Is there?

There is another knock

Bobby Yeah.

Idris I didn't hear anything.

Gran (*calling*) Idris!

Idris Funny. I only had my ears syringed yesterday.

Bobby Perhaps it's ver wind.

Idris No, I only get that in my stomach.

Gran Idris, answer the door, will you?

Bobby (*looking towards the ceiling*) There's somebody calling you now, as well.

Idris (*putting his fingers to his ears*) I must be going deaf.

The door is knocked again, harder this time

Bobby (*standing*) Shall I answer it?

Idris Yes. If you would.

Bobby goes to the door. Idris picks up the mugs of tea from the floor, puts them on the table then goes to sit in the armchair

Tracy They must be hard of hearing down there.
Gran You don't 'ave to tell me. I shout my bloody 'ead off up 'ere, that's all I do. I wonder who it is?

Maisie Millard enters

Maisie Hello.
Bobby Hello. Who are you?
Maisie Mrs Millard. From next door. I'll go through.

Maisie Millard enters like a tornado. She is wearing an overall. No tights and fluffy mule-type slippers. She has one hair roller in. She carries a magazine

Hello, Idris. How are you?
Idris (*putting his right hand to his forehead*) Oh, I'm not too good, I——
Maisie (*sitting on a chair by the table*) Where's Elsie and Tracy then?

With his hand still on his forehead. Idris indicates upstairs with his other hand. He holds this position until his next line

Idris Well, Tracy's upstairs and Elsie's——
Maisie (*putting the magazine on the arm of the settee*) I've brought a magazine for what's-her-name.

She turns to Bobby who has come to stand L of the settee

Well, you must be Bobby, Tracy's boy.
Bobby That's right, yeah, I'm——
Maisie (*to Idris*) Elsie gone visiting, has she?
Idris (*still pointing towards the ceiling he indicates with his other hand, pointing his thumb down* R) Gone to see her sister Dot, she's——
Maisie Having her sinus done.
Idris (*still indicating with his right hand he points to his nose with his left index finger*) Do you know I'm still waiting to hear about——
Maisie What are you celebrating then? I can see you've been drinking.
Idris (*putting his two hands in front of him, palms down*) Well, we're not celebrating anything, really, are we——
Maisie Is it gin I can smell? Do you know I haven't drunk gin since my wedding night.
Idris Well, do you fancy a——
Maisie Oh, I shouldn't really but—go on then.
Idris Bobby?
Bobby Yes, please, Mr Roberts.

Idris takes the two empty glasses and makes for the sideboard. Bobby is also on his way to join him. Suddenly they are both stopped in their tracks by Maisie Millard's line

Maisie I hope it won't bring back memories, Idris.

Idris and Bobby look at each other, then at Maisie Millard

Idris (*enquiring tentatively*) Wasn't it a night to remember, then?
Maisie (*shaking her head but not looking at them*) I'd rather not talk about it, Idris, if you don't mind.

Idris and Bobby look at each other again then carry on preparing the drinks. There is a slight pause

Idris (*to Maisie*) Tonic?

Maisie No, I never mix my drinks.

During the following short scene, Idris pours the drinks, gives one to Bobby and is at the table in time for his cue. Bobby takes his drink and sits on the settee

Gran It's all gone quiet now.

Tracy I wonder who it was. It can't be Mammy, (*looking at her watch*) it's too early for her yet.

Gran That's what plays on me more than anything being up 'ere; I don't know what's going on down there.

Tracy Listen, I'm sure I can hear a woman's voice.

Tracy and Gran lean heavily to the left, like two budgies on a perch

Maisie (*grabbing Idris' arm in an intensive manner*) No, I'm not being funny to you Idris, I'm not being funny. But to talk about it would hurt too much.

Idris (*trying to loosen her grip*) Even after all this time?

Maisie (*hurt*) It's only fourteen years.

Idris hands her the drink

Thank you. Cheers everybody.

Bobby and Maisie drink as Idris makes his way to the armchair. As he does this he loses his balance and sways a little

Are you all right Idris?

Idris Oh . . . I nearly went then! I'd better sit down. I think it's my vertigo. (*He sits*)

There is a pause in which Maisie stares at Idris intensely. He becomes aware of this and very slowly meets her gaze. She immediately looks away

Maisie No, I never talk about my wedding night, because it still upsets me.

Idris nods then looks away. He sips his drink but is still aware of Maisie staring again. Awkwardly he looks at her again and she pounces

I just don't talk about it at all.

Idris looks at Bobby then out front. Maisie now turns to Bobby who slowly becomes aware of her gaze and meets her eye

Well, not very much anyway. (*She looks front*) Only sometimes. (*After a pause*) If someone will listen.

There is a pause. Action upstairs

Gran I can't 'ear a thing now.

Tracy It's like the grave.

They both straighten up

Gran I wonder if Nobby 'ave told 'im yet?

Tracy I expect he has by now. I wonder what Daddy have said.

Gran I can still remember what *my* father said. He was 'aving 'is food at the time. Broth it was. My mother was there too, darning 'is socks by the fire. Oh, it took ages for your grandfather to pluck up courage to tell *my* father I was in trouble. Finally he came out with it anyway. My father stopped chewing for a minute, he let the words sink in, then he 'alf turned 'is 'ead to my mother and he said "These carrots are 'ard," he said. (*She laughs*) He didn't 'ave any teeth see, poor bugger.

Action downstairs

Maisie You'll have to promise not to laugh then. Idris?

Idris I promise.

Maisie Bobby?

Bobby Yeah, promise.

Maisie Well ... it was about eleven o'clock. No, I tell a lie, it was twelve o'clock ... Wait a minute. (*She thinks for a moment*) I'll start again. It was one o'clock in the morning, right?

Idris Right.

Bobby Right.

Maisie Right. (*Holding out her glass*) Hey, do you think I could have another one of these?

Idris Yes, of course. Bobby, fill Maisie's glass.

Bobby gets the bottle of gin and fills the glass

Maisie It's funny, but gin is like a dictionary to me, Idris. The more I drink, the more words I got.

Idris Well, I tell you what. Have a chapter on me.

Maisie (*laughing*) Ooh, I didn't know you had a sense of humour Idris?

Idris Nor me. I thought I had it out with my tonsils.

Maisie (*screaming with laugher*) Tonsils!!

Idris and Bobby join in the laughter

Action upstairs

Gran Do you 'ear that laughter?

Tracy Yeah, things must be all right.

Gran There *is* a woman down there.

Tracy Perhaps it's Mammy after all.

Gran (*shaking her head*) No. There's only one woman who laughs like that.

Tracy Maisie Millard.

Gran Right first time.

Tracy What do she want?

Gran I often ask myself that question Tracy, and I always come back with the same answer.

Tracy What's that?

Gran Your father.

Tracy But she's got a husband.
Gran He don't "bother" with 'er.
Tracy What do you mean?
Gran He only 'ad 'er once, before they were married. Rumour 'as it he haven't touched 'er since.
Tracy So that's why Jeffrey's an only child.
Gran Well, of course.
Tracy (*after thinking a moment*) I'm an only child, Gran.
Gran Yes, but I've told you. Your father was advised by the doctor not to 'ave any more children. 'Er 'usband advised 'imself.

Action downstairs

Maisie Well anyway ... I'd gone to bed before Bernard. He was still downstairs talking to my father. It was about three-quarters of an hour after that he managed to get away. They don't bloody talk to one another now but trust my father to keep him talking on our wedding night. I was sitting on the ottoman when he came into the room; I was combing my hair and he looked over at me, oh and I knew he wanted me because he'd turned this funny colour puce. He always looks like that when he's aroused. I put my comb down on the utility dressing table—and he just stared at me. I smiled back at him, and then I started to shiver—with sheer delight. (*Excited*) I told you gin gives me words, didn't I? Now, where was I?
Bobby (*eagerly*) You started to shiver.
Maisie That's right.
Idris (*just as excited*) With sheer delight.
Maisie I could feel the passion oozing out of the pupils of his eyes. He'd kicked the door closed as he undone his belt. My breathing was beginning to quicken; suddenly, they fell to his ankles.
Bobby What did?
Idris His pupils?
Maisie No, his trousers. He stepped out of them as he kicked them to one side. He just stood there—naked.
Bobby (*after a pause*) What 'appened to 'is shirt?
Idris Sshhhh!
Maisie He had such a magnificent body. I stood up. (*She does*) I'd left the top of the bedroom window open and a soft breeze came in and gently shook my nightie. This moved him. He took one careful step towards me. (*She takes one step forward*) His huge feet were spread like magnificent webbed things on the floor. We didn't have lino then. We couldn't stay apart any longer; his arms held out for my touch; and as he was running towards me—it happened.
Idris ⎫ (*together*) What did?
Bobby ⎭
Maisie His foot went through the bloody floorboard. I can still see his face now.
Bobby The pain.
Maisie The disappointment.

Idris (*grimacing*) The splinters.
Maisie He's still taking them out. (*She turns back to the chair*) Our marriage haven't been the same since. (*She sits*) But I don't like to talk about it.

Action upstairs

Gran Course she fancied your father once.
Tracy Did she?
Gran There was a 'ell of a row about it 'ere at one time. Just before a Christmas, it was. Me and your mother 'ad gone Christmas shopping and we said we wouldn't be back 'til four, but the shops were so crowded we decided to come 'ome early.
Tracy What happened?
Gran I won't go into the details, but your father 'ave still got a scar to mark the occasion.
Tracy There were fireworks then?
Gran (*nodding her head*) Oh, your mother 'ave got 'ell of a temper. She was sorry after, mind, because it was innocent; but she's never trusted your father and Maisie Millard ever since.

During Gran's last line, Bobby has picked up the magazine that Maisie brought in

Bobby This 'ere, is it?
Maisie Yes, that's it. She'll enjoy looking through that.
Bobby All right if I take it up, Mr Roberts?
Idris Yes, carry on.

Bobby leaves the room and goes upstairs

As soon as he is out of sight, Maisie takes out her hair roller. She then takes a bottle of perfume from her pocket and sprays herself. She takes her glass and the bottle to the settee. She clinks them to get Idris' attention

Maisie Shall I fill you up again, Idris?
Idris (*looking at his empty glass*) Why not?
Maisie Come over here then.

He joins her

    Not a lot left now.
Idris Finish it off then.
Maisie Are you sure?
Idris (*sitting next to her*) Yes.

Maisie fills his glass

    He's not a bad kid, is he? I reckon our Tracy could do a lot worse. (*He sips his gin*)
Maisie Oh, our Jeffrey thinks he's lovely.

Idris almost chokes

    Upstairs, Bobby knocks on the bedroom door

Gran Who's that?
Tracy It's open.

Bobby comes in

Oh, hello. (*To Gran*) It's Bobby.
Gran Who?
Tracy Bobby. My boyfriend.
Bobby 'Ow be.
Gran (*mimicking him*) 'Ow be.
Bobby 'Ow you keeping?
Gran (*still mimicking*) Not so bad, see.
Tracy Sit down.

Bobby sits

Gran (*to Tracy*) Ugly bugger, isn't he?
Bobby (*showing the magazine*) I brought you vis, look.
Gran What is it?
Bobby A magazine.
Gran Is it dirty?
Bobby (*not sure*) I don't fink so.
Gran I don't want it then. (*She cackles*) Go on, I'm only pulling your leg.

Bobby suddenly realizes the joke and laughs. Gran makes a face at Tracy

Bobby It's from the woman next door. Mrs ... er ... Mi ...
Gran (*surprised*) Maisie Millard?
Bobby That's 'er.
Gran (*immediately taking it from him*) I bet it is dirty then. Let's 'ave a look. (*She turns a few pages*) Oh, she shouldn't send me these, not with my 'igh blood pressure.
Tracy It's not dirty, is it.
Gran (*viewing the magazine at various angles*) You got to be a contamonist to get into 'alf of these positions. (*Throwing it to the bottom of the bed*) Nothing's ever the same, is it? Even sex is different these days. Not like when I was a girl. Women knew their places in those days. In those days, she went under the blanket—he went under the thumb.

Action downstairs

Idris I don't quite know how to tell you this, Maisie.
Maisie If you've got something on your chest, Idris it's best to get it out—in the open.
Idris I don't know how to start.
Maisie (*beginning to stroke his knee*) You'll feel a lot better once you've got it off your chest.
Idris I want to talk to you about it.
Maisie (*putting her arm around his back*) About what?
Idris But it's not easy for me to say. I mean, I don't really know how to handle the situation.
Maisie (*excited*) What situation, Idris?

Idris (*standing*) You see, I've always had this feeling

Maisie stands close to him and he holds her hand to his chest

this feeling deep down inside, that one day it was going to happen to me.
(*He becomes emotional*) And now it has.

Maisie What has?

Idris (*getting carried away*) It's not fair for it to happen now. Not at my time
of life. I'm a married man with responsibilities. I'm too young to——

Maisie Oh Idris. (*Stroking his hair*) You don't mean that . . . me . . . and
you . . .

Idris I've tried not to think about it, but it's no use. (*He sits on the arm of the
settee*)

Maisie (*standing behind him, hands on his shoulders*) I always knew you had
feelings for me.

Idris How will Elsie manage without me?

Maisie (*kneeling in front of him*) There's no need for us to elope.

Idris And there's Tracy to consider.

Maisie Oh, we shouldn't tell them.

Idris They already know.

Maisie (*standing*) Never!

Idris (*crying*) Yes. (*Taking her hand*) Oh, Maisie, Maisie. What am I going
to do?

Maisie Well, for now, just lay back and enjoy it. (*She pushes him back on to
the settee then jumps on top of him*)

Idris (*from underneath*) Get off . . . get off . . .

Maisie Don't fight it Idris.

Idris I can't breathe.

Maisie (*almost suffocating him*) This thing between us is bigger than you or
me.

Idris (*struggling*) I can't breathe. Get up. Let me get up. (*He manages to get
away from her*)

Maisie You're a real man, Idris.

Idris I'm not well.

Maisie Don't run away. Come here.

Idris No, no. You don't understand. I'm a sick man and I haven't got long.

Maisie (*chasing him*) I know. So let's get on with it before Elsie comes back
from the hospital.

She chases him across the room. They end up either side of the settee

Idris What about Tracy?

Maisie What about her?

Idris She's upstairs. And think of Bernard.

Maisie (*taking off her shoes and throwing them over her shoulders*) To hell
with Bernard.

*She chases him across the room again. He picks up a dining-room chair and
holds it in front of him*

Idris Pull yourself together.

Maisie I've always wanted you Idris. For years I've thought of nothing else.
Idris But I'm a sick man.
Maisie (*slowly moving to centre stage*) I'll nurse you.
Idris I don't want you to nurse me.
Maisie Love me, then. Love me now!! (*She tears off her overall and has only her underwear on*)
Idris Oh my God!

He throws down the chair and runs into the kitchen. Maisie follows him

Action upstairs

Gran Where are you going to live, have you decided?
Tracy } (*together*) { With my mother.
Bobby } (*together*) { With my father.
Tracy I'm not living with your father.
Bobby And I'm not living 'ere, neither.
Gran What's the matter with living 'ere, then?
Bobby When she's my wife, she'll live where I tell 'er to.
Tracy (*shouting*) Will I? If you think I'm going to keep house for your family, Bobby, you can think again.
Gran That's right, love, you tell 'im. No granddaughter of mine is going to be put on like that.
Bobby You keep out of this. This is between me and Deborah.
Tracy } (*together*) Who's Deborah?
Gran }
Bobby I mean Tracy.
Tracy It's that girl who comes in for three-star, isn't it?
Bobby Don't be daft.
Gran He's not knocking about with somebody else, is he? (*To Bobby*) I swear I'll kill you if you are. (*She hits him with her pillow*)
Tracy (*upset*) You've always liked her.
Bobby I don't know who you're talking about.
Tracy That girl with the red hair.
Bobby I said the wrong name, that's all.
Tracy Wrong name! Well, that's it as far as I'm concerned. It's all off. We're finished.
Bobby (*standing*) Fair enough then.

He storms out

Action downstairs

Bobby enters the hallway

Elsie comes in through the front door and meets him

Idris is chased from kitchen to living-room by Maisie. His shirt is torn open and he is hanging on to his trousers

Maisie I want you.
Idris No.

Maisie Kiss me.
Idris I'll tell Bernard.
Maisie I don't care.
Idris (*calling*) Help.
Maisie Let me help you off with your shirt.
Idris No.
Maisie Your trousers, then.
Idris Help!
Elsie (*screaming*) Idris!!!

Idris turns around to see Elsie, looks back at Maisie. His trousers fall to his ankles and he faints

Black-out

CURTAIN

ACT III

The same. Late morning, the following day

When the CURTAIN *rises Tracy is sitting at the dining-table writing a letter. Gran lies awake in bed. She is motionless. After some time she sighs heavily then speaks*

Gran Oh, the days are awful long up 'ere. It's too quiet. It's like the grave. Perhaps it is the grave. Perhaps I've died and gone to 'eaven. No, this can't be 'eaven; they'd 'ave nicer wallpaper than this up there. I wonder if it's the other place? Although, what I've done to go there I don't know. (*She feels her arms*) I don't feel dead. I wonder if you know when you're dead or 'ave someone got to come and tell you. (*Calling*) Elsie? Elsie? Come and tell me if I'm dead, will you? (*She cackles then sighs again*) Oh, I'm awful bored. (*She pauses as she looks around the room. Eventually, her eyes fall on the chair next to her bed. She addresses it*) 'Scuse me. You don't mind if I talk to you, do you? Only some chairs are funny; they don't like it; but I've got to talk to somebody or I'll go off my bloody 'ead up 'ere. (*A slight pause*) I made friends with a moth the other day. (*Pointing off* R) Over there he was on the window sill. I spoke to 'im for three weeks—then it dawned on me he 'adn't moved. Passed on. I don't know if he caught a cold from the draught in the window and died—or if I talked the bugger to death. I've made friends with a fly now though. Comes in to see me every day; but I don't like 'im; he's sly. Flies are like that though, aren't they? Devious. I was talking to 'im this morning and under my nose he went and landed on the rim of my cocoa cup. Well, I couldn't drink my cocoa after that, could I (*A slight pause*) He 'aven't been well, mind. He's going down with the flu I think. (*She cackles*) A fly with the flu. "Go downstairs and 'ave a warm by the fire—it's bloody freezing up 'ere," I said. I told our Elsie "I want a fire up 'ere," I said. I get chilly in the nights. But she won't let me 'ave one. Says she can't afford it—but it's not that—she just don't trust me. Can't say I blame 'er. Mind you, it's a bit better up 'ere now. Some little man came and put stuff down in the attic. I fancy there's a big difference now they've 'ad the roof insulted. (*She catches sight of a fly*) Oh, talk of the devil—look who just flew in. 'Ello. 'Ow are you? Are you better? Well, you're looking better (*To the chair*) I got to tell 'im that see, 'cause I want to ask 'im a favour after. (*To the fly*) I was just saying, you 'aven't been well, have you? (*A slight pause*) What else is the matter with you then? A 'eadache? (*To the chair*) He's getting like our Idris he is. Always something wrong with 'im. (*To the fly*) Well I'd 'ave a 'eadache if I didn't stop making that infernal buzzing, and keep still when I'm talking to you. 'Ow long 'ave you 'ad that 'eadache? Eh? Well, go and ask our Idris for two Panadols, that'll put you right. (*To the chair*) I know what it's like to suffer with your 'ead. (*To the fly*) Do as I say now and . . . well, where the 'ell 'ave he gone now? (*She looks around the room but doesn't spot him. She is about to give up the search when she sees him on her mug*) There he is look. Oye! I told you this morning, you are not to sit on Gran's cocoa cup. Come on. (*To the chair*) He won't listen to me see. (*To the fly*) 'Ey, you. I was just telling this chair now that . . . (*She faces front*) 'Ell, I just thought of something. (*Pointing scornfully to the fly*) Don't you go downstairs and tell them I've been talking to a bloody chair, mind. They'll be putting me away; only a chance our Elsie is looking for—I know that. (*To the chair*) She would, see, I know 'er. (*To the fly*) So, you listen to what I'm . . . well 'ell, he's gone again. (*She looks around the room and spots him in mid-flight*) There he is look. (*To the fly*) 'Ey come down 'ere, I want to ask you a favour. No, I'm not talking to you when you're flying about up there. Come 'ere to me. (*She holds out the back of her hand*) Come on. Come on to me. (*The fly lands on her hand*) There you are. (*To the chair*) There he is look. (*To the fly*) Say 'ello to the chair. Listen now, will you do me a favour? Will you go downstairs and see if they've left me in this 'ouse on my own self. Will you? Oh, go on, it won't take you two minutes to fly down there. You won't? You're not going to do it for me? Are you sure, 'cause you'll be awful sorry, mind? Last chance. Will you go? You won't? Right then. (*She slaps the back of her hand and kills him. She rubs the back of her hand in the blankets as she speaks*) That'll teach 'im to be bloody spiteful!

There is a knock on the door

Somebody at the door. Idris! Tracy!
Tracy (*calling up the stairs*) It's all right, I heard it.
Gran Tell Gran who it is.

Tracy answers the door

Bobby is there

Tracy Oh, it's you.
Bobby Can I come in?
Gran Tracy, who is it?

Tracy goes into the living-room. Bobby follows her. Tracy stands R of the settee, Bobby L

Tracy I didn't expect to see you today.
Bobby I come round in my dinner hour. I fought we'd better 'ave a chat.
Tracy I hope you've come round to apologize. I didn't get a wink of sleep last night, you upset me so much. I finally cried myself off about half-past four, but it wasn't until I'd soaked the pillow; and I shouldn't get upset, not like that, not in my condition. (*A slight pause*) Well, come on. What have you got to say? What have you got to say to me?
Bobby (*with difficulty*) I love you!
Tracy (*beginning to cry*) Oh, Bobby!
Bobby What have I said now?

They sit on the settee

Tracy I'm sorry.
Bobby For what?
Tracy For calling it off. Can I call it back on again?
Bobby Course you can.
Tracy It was my fault. I should never have done it.
Bobby Forget about it, Trace.
Tracy So it's back on then?

Bobby nods

When shall it be?
Bobby I don't know.
Tracy I thought perhaps next month. The fifteenth.
Bobby Vat's a Saturday, is it?
Tracy (*nodding*) Everyone gets married on a Saturday.
Bobby Fair enough then.

There is a pause

About where we'd live.
Tracy Oh, I haven't got to go and live in your house, have I?
Bobby Not if you don't want to.
Tracy That's all right then.
Bobby I just fought you might want to. Under ver circumstances.
Tracy (*after a slight pause*) What circumstances?
Bobby Well, it's my father, see.
Tracy What about him?
Bobby I 'aven't told you before but ... well ... he's not very well.
Tracy You mean he's ill.
Bobby He's always 'ad a cronky 'eart. It's only a matter of time—about a year or so.
Tracy (*beginning to cry*) Oh, Bobby.
Bobby But we don't 'ave to go and live there if you don't want to.
Tracy Oh, no I want to, I want to.
Bobby We'll come and live 'ere if you like.
Tracy (*drying her eyes*) No, I'd rather live in your house.
Bobby Are you sure?
Tracy Yes.
Bobby Fair enough then.

There is a slight pause

Tracy Does he know?
Bobby Who?
Tracy Your father.
Bobby About what?
Tracy His heart.
Bobby Oh, yeah.
Tracy I'll be able to look after him.

Bobby Yeah, he'd like that Trace.

Tracy How long has he got, did you say?

Bobby Not long, only about a year.

Tracy Who will he leave the house to, I wonder?

Bobby It's rented.

Tracy (*tutting*) Shame. (*After a slight pause*) Did you tell my father last night?

Bobby Yeah.

Tracy What did he say?

Bobby He didn't say anyfing. Oh, wait a minute, yes he did. He said he knew.

Tracy He knew?

Bobby He said he knew it was only a matter of time.

Tracy (*a little hurt*) Well, that's not very nice.

Bobby I fought it was great. I didn't 'ave to tell 'im anyfing; he more or less put it together 'imself. "Consider the matter said," he said.

Tracy That doesn't sound like my father to me.

Bobby Well, that's what he said Trace, 'onest. Where is he anyway?

Tracy In bed. He hasn't come down this morning yet. My mother was off her head. Mrs Millard have been after my father for years. According to Gran they were caught together once before.

Bobby What 'appened then?

Tracy I don't know the details but she got off lucky this time.

Bobby Good job I came in when I did then.

Tracy I had to hide the breadknife.

Bobby She wouldn't 'ave used it, would she?

Tracy All I know is if you hadn't taken it from her when you did—two minutes later you would have been taking it out of Mrs Millard's back. (*She rises and puts the writing pad and pen in the sideboard drawer*)

Bobby I told *my* father last night.

Tracy What did he say?

Bobby Not much.

Tracy What do you mean "not much"?

Bobby He just gave me a 'ammering.

Tracy I thought you said he was a sick man.

Bobby He is. That's why I couldn't 'it 'im back.

Tracy I can't think why he hit you.

Bobby I can.

Tracy For getting me into trouble.

Bobby No, for not using anyfing.

Tracy comes to sit next to Bobby on the settee

Tracy (*after a pause*) I know perhaps it's wrong, right? But I thought I might go in white.

Bobby (*after a slight pause*) Go where in white?

Tracy To the chapel?

Bobby You mean 'ave a really wedding?

Tracy I don't fancy the Registry Office and I've always wanted to get married in white.
Bobby Ay, but who's going to pay, Trace?
Tracy I don't think it would cost *that* much more than if we went quiet.
Bobby Ay, but who's going to pay?
Tracy My father.
Bobby Well, you can tell 'im then, OK?
Tracy It might bring on another coronary—but I'll chance it.
Bobby Mind you, saying that—I've only got a small family, Trace; only about sixteen at ver most.
Tracy Mine's not much more; about eighteen.
Bobby Well, vat's not bad, is it (*Making a quick mental addition*) Fifty-free!
Tracy It's settled then—I'll go in white.

There is a knock at the front door

Gran Somebody at the door!
Tracy (*getting up*) I'll get it.
Bobby (*pushing her back*) No, you stay there, I'll go. (*He goes to the door*)
Gran Tracy? Answer the door somebody.

Maisie is at the front door

Maisie (*sheepishly*) Hello Bobby.
Bobby Hello.
Gran 'Ave you answered it?
Maisie I'll go through.

Bobby is about to follow Maisie into the living-room but is stopped by Gran

Gran (*calling*) 'Ave anybody answered that door?
Bobby (*shouting from the bottom of the stairs*) Yes.
Gran Who's that, Idris?
Bobby No, Bobby.
Maisie (*standing L of the settee*) Hello Tracy.
Gran Who did you say?
Tracy My mother's not here.
Bobby (*shouting*) Bobby!
Maisie (*sitting L on the settee*) Where is she then?
Gran Who was at the door?
Tracy I think she's down my auntie's.
Bobby (*still at the bottom of the stairs*) Mrs Millard.
Gran (*screaming*) Mrs Millard?
Maisie (*half-rising from her seat as she calls to Bobby*) Do you want me?
Tracy No, he's shouting to Gran.
Maisie Oh ... (*laughing*) ... I thought he was calling me.
Gran Did you let 'er in?
Bobby Yes.
Gran Well, throw the bugger back out then.
Maisie Where's your father?
Tracy In bed.

Gran Do you 'ear me, Noddy?

Maisie Not well, is he?

Tracy His nerves are bad. (*To Bobby*) Leave her Bobby or she'll have you standing there all day.

Bobby crosses from the hall and enters the living-room. He stands behind the settee

Gran Can you 'ear me down there?

Tracy (*to Bobby*) What does she want, anyway?

Bobby (*putting his hands on the back of the settee as he leans forward slightly, nodding to Maisie*) She wants me to frow 'er out.

Maisie Oh, don't do that, Bobby. (*She puts her hand on his*)

Bobby (*immediately pulling his hand away*) Hey! (*He looks at her with disdain and goes to sit next to Tracy at the dining-table*)

Maisie Is there any chance of your father getting up? I'd like to explain to him.

Tracy It's not my father you want to see, it's my mother.

Maisie When are you expecting her back?

Tracy I don't know.

Maisie It was all that drink, see. I'm not used to it. I didn't know what I was doing. (*Trying to explain*) It was the gin. It makes my blood go red hot and Idris should never have forced it on me.

Tracy Perhaps you'd better call in and see her again.

Maisie Yes, I suppose you're right. Have she cooled down yet?

Gran Sort 'er out Tracy.

Tracy No.

Maisie Better leave it 'til she has then. When do you think would be the best time to call?

Tracy (*shrugging her shoulders*) One day next year.

Gran *I* ought to be down there now.

Maisie I *would* like to see your father though, to explain.

Tracy *I'll* explain for you.

Maisie Will you? Tell him I didn't mean it. I didn't know what I was doing. (*She crosses behind Bobby, stops momentarily and rests her hands on his shoulders*)

Bobby stiffens

Tell him it was the drink, it affects me that way. Tell him I'd been depressed and I hadn't eaten all day. (*She loses control of her emotions*) Tell him I was drunk and that I'm sorry—I got carried away (*she cries*) and that I'm a very emotional woman.

At this moment Idris appears at the bottom of the stairs. He has just got up from bed and is wearing a surgical collar

And he shouldn't go looking at me with those pitiful eyes and ... oh ... I'm getting upset. (*She sits in the armchair and dries her eyes with the corner of her apron*)

Tracy looks at Bobby then looks L where she sees Idris

Tracy Oh, Dad.
Maisie (*looking up*) Oh, Idris.
Idris (*seeing Maisie*) Oh, hell. (*He starts to leave the room*)

But Tracy and Bobby catch him and bring him back in and sit him down on the settee. He struggles but they eventually calm him down

Tracy Sit down, Dad, you're all right.
Maisie I've only come to talk to you.
Gran Don't listen to a word she says Tracy.
Tracy (*sitting Idris on the settee*) There you are, you're all right.

Bobby now moves to the table and sits in the chair R. *Tracy is standing* L *of the settee, her right arm firmly gripped by Idris*

Idris (*to Tracy*) You won't leave me, will you?
Maisie (*to Idris*) I've only come to apologize.
Gran If she's come to apologize, don't accept.
Idris Go and lock the front door Tracy. If your mother comes back now—I am a dead man.
Maisie (*half-rising from the chair*) I only want to explain to you.
Idris (*shouting at her*) Well explain from where you are and then go out the back way.

Maisie sits again

Tracy Relax, Dad. Everything will be all right.
Maisie (*to Tracy*) He's awful edgy, isn't he?
Tracy Yeah, it's my mother.
Idris (*panic-stricken*) Where? (*He almost jumps out of his seat and makes everybody jump*)
Tracy (*holding Idris down by his shoulders*) All this have made his nerves bad.
Maisie (*still shaken*) See if you can calm him down a bit.
Idris (*to Maisie*) I'll be all right once you've gone.
Maisie Give him a drink or something.
Idris (*shouting*) No . . . no, I don't want anything alcoholic.
Maisie I meant tea, Idris
Tracy Do you fancy a cup, Dad?
Idris Yes, all right.

Tracy moves towards the kitchen. Idris holds on to her firmly

No, don't you make it. You stay here with me.
Maisie What's the matter with you Idris? I'm not going to eat you.
Idris Maybe not. But you'll have a bloody good try. (*To Tracy*) Let Bobby do it.
Tracy (*to Bobby*) Will you?

Bobby looks at his oily hands then looks at Tracy and nods

Everything should be on the table; if you can't find anything, give me a shout.

Bobby goes to the kitchen, scratching his backside as he goes

Maisie (*watching him go*) Oh, he's awful good, isn't he?

Idris (*tapping the seat next to him on the settee*) Come and sit by me.

Maisie (*as if ejected from her seat*) All right.

Idris (*shouting*) No ... not you! I was talking to Tracy.

Maisie returns to her seat, disappointed. Tracy sits next to Idris. Maisie sighs, followed by Tracy, followed by Idris, followed by Gran who sighs harder than the other three. There is a pause. Maisie breaks it

Maisie Having anything new for the wedding, Tracy?

Idris
Tracy } (*together, looking at her*) What wedding?

Maisie Well, if rumours are anything to go by, Bobby's brother is getting married. Isn't that right, Tracy?

Tracy (*looking uncomfortable*) Not that I know of.

Maisie Oh, go on—you may as well tell me, half the place is talking about it already.

During the next few lines Idris begins to feel the glands in the side of his throat. He also puts his fingers to his temples

Tracy Well, I haven't heard anything.

Maisie You mean they haven't invited you? Oh well, perhaps it's early days yet. (*A slight pause*) They say there's a little one on the way too.

Tracy (*trying to smile*) Do they?

Maisie Mind you, I'm not surprised. He was a wicked little bugger at the best of times.

Tracy I don't think it's true or Bobby would have said something.

Maisie Well, there must be something in it. What do you say, Idris?

Idris (*feeling his forehead*) I don't feel very well.

Tracy (*impatiently*) What's the matter with *you* now?

Idris I think I'm going to pass out. (*He does*)

Maisie (*catapulting out of her chair*) Oh, don't do that. (*She rushes to him and stands behind the settee and leans over him*) Quick, Tracy, send for the doctor.

Tracy (*who has seen it all before*) There's no need.

Maisie (*cupping his head in her hands she holds his head back to get a better view of him*) Oh, my God ... he's gone ... he's gone. (*Panicking*) Look at his colour, ... he's chalk. Perhaps we should undo his shirt.

Idris makes guttural noises as he grabs the front of his shirt with his two fists

What did he say?

Tracy (*unconcerned*) Come on, Dad. You're all right.

Maisie (*slapping the back of Idris' hands to loosen his grip*) He doesn't look all right to me. Hasn't he got any tablets?

Tracy Of course he has but I don't know which ones to give him.

Idris (*mumbling*) Blue ones.

Tracy And I don't know where they are.

Idris (*mumbling*) Bathroom.
Maisie Bathroom.
Tracy (*turning to leave*) Bathroom.
Maisie That's right, you have a look for them—and I'll give him the kiss of
  life.

She brings her mouth almost down on his as Idris screams and comes to

Idris Where am I?
Tracy I thought that might bring him round.
Idris (*panicking again*) I ... I've gone blind ... I can't see.

Maisie slowly fits his glasses back over his eyes. He relaxes

  Oh!
Maisie Are you all right, Idris?
Idris Yes ... yes.
Maisie (*smoothing the top of his head*) You had a turn. I thought we'd lost
  you. Thought you'd passed on.
Tracy How do you feel now, Dad?
Idris I'm all right.
Tracy Do you want me to fetch your tablets?
Idris No ... no ... I'm all right.
Maisie Good. You shall have a nice cup of tea, now. (*She moves back across
  to the armchair*)
Idris I don't know what came over me.
Maisie I know. I felt exactly the same last night.
Idris Suddenly, everything went dark.
Maisie That's right. (*She sits*) And you don't know what you're doing, do
  you. Well, I didn't anyway. Oh by the way, while I remember. (*She stands
  and takes three shirt buttons from her pocket*) Here's three of your shirt
  buttons I pulled off last night. I don't know what happened to the rest.
  (*She crosses to them*)

*Idris backs up against the arm of the settee as she approaches. She gives the
buttons to Tracy*

  You take them Tracy and put them somewhere safe. (*She returns to her
  seat*) You're sure you're all right now, Idris?
Idris I feel a little faint, that's all.

Dishes are heard smashing in the kitchen

Tracy (*rising*) I think I'd better go and help Bobby.
Idris No! Don't leave me.
Tracy I'm only going to the kitchen.
Idris But what if your mother——
Tracy Call me if you want anything.

  Tracy goes off to the kitchen

Maisie It's all right Idris. Don't feel uneasy. I won't get off this chair, I
  promise.

Idris It's just that if Elsie should come ...
Maisie I'll explain it all. That's why I've come in—to explain it to her. Well ... and to you, of course.

There is a pause

Idris You were like a mad woman last night.
Maisie That's what drink does to me.
Idris Somehow we got our wires crossed.
Maisie (*under her breath*) I'd cross wires with you anytime.
Idris What?
Maisie Nothing.
Idris I was trying to tell you something ... and ... well ... you misunderstood it for something else.
Maisie It was the drink ... it was all the drink. I swear I'll never touch you again.
Idris (*sliding to the right of the settee*) I was trying to tell you that ... well ... I know some people think I'm a bit of a hypochondriac ...
Maisie Oh, Idris ...
Idris No, it's true, it's true. I know it's true—I'm aware of that. But the fact of the matter is (*he swallows hard*) I've got some terrible disease.
Maisie (*getting up*) Oh, no.
Idris Yes. I don't know what it is yet, mind; but I do know that it's (*he almost mouths the word*) terminal.
Maisie Oh, my God. (*She puts her apron to her face*)
Idris It'll all be over in eight weeks.
Maisie (*bringing down the apron*) Never!
Idris Incredible, isn't it?
Maisie I can't believe it.
Idris Well, it's right enough, take it from me. I overheard Elsie and Tracy talking about it yesterday.
Maisie She hasn't said a word to me.
Idris Well, no ... she wouldn't.
Maisie And Tracy knows as well?
Idris (*nodding*) I heard them planning for Bobby to come round and tell me last night.
Maisie And did he?
Idris Oh, yes. He got a bit embarrassed about it, of course. Couldn't find the right words, you know. So I had to help him out a bit. "Consider the matter said," I said.
Maisie (*rising and moving towards him*) Oh, Idris!
Idris (*panicking at her advance*) Stay where you are! For God's sake, stay where you are.
Maisie (*returning to her seat*) You seem to be taking it pretty well, anyway.
Idris Well, I've got to haven't I? It's pointless losing your head (*he starts to get upset*) and getting upset about it.
Maisie (*crying, she moves towards him again*) Oh, Idris!
Idris (*shouting*) Stay where you are.
Maisie (*returning to her seat*) You poor thing. And all over in eight weeks.

Idris (*trying to control his emotions*) Yes. But never mind. I'll get over it in a couple of months.

Maisie It's funny how Elsie hasn't said anything, though. And she doesn't seem to be upset at all.

Idris I think she's putting a brave face on it.

Maisie I expect you're right.

Idris She must be upset because she couldn't bring herself to tell me personally. That's why they asked Bobby.

Maisie Of course.

Tracy and Bobby enter from the kitchen carrying two cups each

Tracy Here you are then.

She hands a cup to Idris and keeps one herself. Bobby hands one to Maisie and keeps one himself

Maisie Thank you, Bobby.

Idris Ta, love.

Tracy sits on the settee and Bobby sits by the dining-table

I think I'd better take a tablet, Tracy.

Tracy You fetch them then, because I don't know which ones are which.

Idris I don't know if I can stand.

Tracy Try.

Idris But what about my varicose veins?

Tracy What about them?

Idris (*as he rises and goes to the kitchen*) I don't know. There's no sympathy with youngsters these days. I don't know what's the matter with them. A bloody good kick up the arse they want.

Idris exits to the kitchen

Tracy (*to Maisie*) Tea all right?

Maisie Yes, lovely. (*A slight pause. She sips her tea*) I was sorry to hear about your father.

Bobby and Tracy look at each other, confused. Bobby then assumes she was talking to him and answers

Bobby (*looking at her*) Yeah.

Maisie Sad, isn't it?

Tracy I'd rather go *quick* myself and not know anything about it.

Maisie I wouldn't like to choose between either of them, Tracy. He seems to be taking it pretty well though, doesn't he?

Bobby Oh, he do 'ave 'is low moments, Mrs M.

Maisie Well, that's understandable, Bobby. It takes a brave man who can face the end, that's what I always say. (*After a slight pause*) Well, I think he's marvellous anyway. Not many men would put up with all that tablet taking that he's done over the years.

Bobby and Tracy again exchange puzzled looks

What is it? I mean, I expect you've been told have you, what's wrong with him?

Tracy Yeah, it's his heart, isn't it Bobby?

Bobby Yeah, it's 'is (*emphasizing the apostrophe*) 'eart.

Maisie I've always said it. I've always said I've seen a healthier looking corpse.

Idris enters from the kitchen and moves to L *of the settee, still carrying his cup*

Tracy Did you find them?

Idris Yes, I'm all right now for at least—(*he looks at his watch*)—oh, twenty-five minutes.

Maisie (*quietly; to Bobby*) Sad, isn't it?

There is a pause

Gran (*booming*) Oh, I've 'ad a bloody gutsful up 'ere. (*She stops for a minute then smiles wickedly. She shouts*) Fire! Fire! My room is on fire!

Idris (*listening*) Sshhh. Is that Gran?

Gran That'll shift the buggers.

Idris What's she shouting—fire, is it?

Gran (*cackling*) They'll all be up 'ere now.

Tracy Don't take any notice. She's only shouting for us to go up.

Maisie Or for her to come down.

Gran They must be running for buckets of water.

Maisie It must be awful to be stuck in one room.

Tracy I'd like to see her back down.

Maisie It's not the same down here without her, is it?

Gran (*shouting*) Help! Help! I'm being confumed by the smoke!

Maisie (*looking towards the ceiling*) Perhaps one of you should go and check.

Gran I bet there's pandemonium down there.

They all raise their cups and drink simultaneously. Gran cackles

I bet they're running around like bloody black pats.

They all put their cups back on the saucers

Idris (*to Maisie*) She'd have us going up and down those stairs every five minutes if she had her way.

Gran Funny, I can't 'ear them drawing water.

Maisie My grandmother was the same. She was bedridden for six years.

Gran Perhaps they've sent for the Fire Brigade.

Maisie She outlived my grandfather though.

Gran (*shouting*) Have you sent for the Fire Brigade?

Maisie Going up and down them stairs killed him in the end.

Idris And they will. People don't realize it (*gesturing towards Tracy*) but when you've got a bad heart you avoid steps. That's why Elsie sleeps on the top bunk now.

Maisie (*smiling*) Oh. Got bunk beds have you, Idris?

Idris Yes. (*Almost mouthing*) But don't show.
Gran Nobody seems to be coming up.
Maisie Bernard wanted us to have bunk beds, mind.
Gran They're not leaving me up 'ere, sure to God.
Maisie But if we did, him and Jeffrey would only quarrel over who was to go on top. And then *I'd* have to go and sleep in the bloody box room.
Gran See. I could be smoked to death in my own room and nobody cares.

Tracy rises and goes to Maisie

Tracy Finished with your cup?
Maisie Yes. (*She stands*) I'll take them, go on.
Gran Tracy?
Tracy No, it's all right. I'll do it.
Maisie Come on, give them here, what's the matter with you? It won't take me a minute to swill these, then I'll go out the back way.
Tracy OK then. (*She gives Maisie her cup*)
Gran (*screaming*) Tracy?

Maisie puts the cup on the tray along with Bobby's then goes to Idris

Maisie Idris?
Idris (*looking scared*) I haven't finished yet.
Maisie (*smiling*) Bring it out when you have then.

She winks at him and exits

Gran Will somebody answer me?
Idris God help us Tracy if your mother comes back and catches her doing the dishes.
Tracy (*sitting in the armchair*) Well, it's not my fault. She insisted.
Gran (*booming*) Idris?
Idris (*looking at the ceiling*) She haven't bloody stopped yet, have she?
Bobby I fink she's calling *you* Mr Roberts.
Idris What can I do for her. I'm a sick man myself.
Tracy Why don't you go up for five minutes?
Idris I will after.
Gran I want to come down.
Tracy She's bored, I expect.
Idris The trouble with your grandmother isn't boredom Tracy—it's curiosity.
Gran (*at her wits' end*) Idris, can you 'ear me?
Idris I wish I had her lungs.
Gran (*shouting*) For two pins, I'd wet this bed mind.
Idris I'd be all right if I had a pair like hers.
Gran (*one long continuous scream*) Idriiiiiiiiiiis!!
Tracy There's nothing wrong with your chest.
Gran O, my God ... I have!
Idris What do I take those pink capsules for then?
Gran (*nearly crying*) Oh, no!
Idris Yes. I've got one lung bigger than the other, see Bobby.

Gran Tracy, come quick, will you?
Idris I've seen it with my own eyes. Not that the big one is too big. That's the normal size. It's the other one, Bobby. It's the other one I get trouble with.
Gran Come up somebody. I've wet the bed.
Idris You see, Bobby——

Bobby isn't looking at him

Bobby.

Bobby turns to face him

With one lung smaller, I don't get the same amount of breath as normal people.

Bobby looks away

Gran (*shouting*) I'm soaking!
Idris Therefore my intake of oxygen is lower, which makes my heart, see Bobby——(*He realizes he doesn't have Bobby's attention*) Bobby.

Bobby looks at him

Which makes my heart, see Bobby, work harder and that in turn causes me to have all my coronaries.
Gran (*crying again*) Tracy!
Bobby You seem to know an awful lot about medicine, Mr Roberts.
Idris Oh, I could have been a doctor if I'd wanted to, Bobby.
Tracy But his psychiatrist wouldn't let him.
Idris (*to Tracy*) I didn't like the paper work.
Gran What the 'ell am I going to do now?
Idris (*to Bobby*) *And* my health was against me.
Gran I wish Elsie was 'ere. (*Taking out her black hat from under the blankets she holds it up between thumb and forefinger*)
Tracy I'm as likely to be a cordon bleu cook, as you were to ever become a doctor.
Gran It's all that shouting that 'ave done it.
Idris At the age of twelve, I knew more about medicine than anyone else on my psychiatric wing. Yes, there's not much medically I don't know about.

The front door slams

Gran (*sitting bolt upright*) Who was that?
Idris (*in a panic*) Someone just came in.
Tracy I didn't hear anything.
Gran (*shouting*) 'Ave somebody just come in?
Idris (*shouting*) It's your mother.
Tracy (*rising*) Keep calm.
Gran (*shouting*) Or 'ave somebody just gone out?
Idris (*losing control*) It is . . . it's her, I know it is.
Tracy Calm down and stop shaking.
Idris What am I going to tell her?

Tracy It'll be all right.
Gran (*calling*) Who is it?

Elsie enters carrying a plastic carrier bag

Tracy Hiya, Mam.
Elsie Hiya. Hello Bobby.
Bobby 'Ow be.

Elsie stands behind the settee and puts the carrier bag on the settee

Tracy What have you got? Something nice?
Elsie I'll show you now.
Gran (*calling*) Is that you Elsie?
Elsie (*noticing that Idris' cup and saucer are rattling*) Somebody's nerves are bad!
Idris (*to Elsie*) Oh, you are speaking to me then?
Elsie (*looking away*) Did something speak?
Gran (*calling*) Elsie?
Elsie I've just been to see Auntie Thelma and Sharon was there too, so I asked her ...

Idris has been nodding his head to try to get Tracy to go into the kitchen and get rid of Maisie. Elsie catches him just as his head is at an awkward angle

What the hell's the matter with you?
Idris (*improvising*) Oh ... er ... I've got a stiff neck. I must have slept awkward.
Elsie Sure it's not rigor mortis?
Idris (*concerned*) Do you think it might be Bobby?
Bobby (*nodding*) Yeah.
Idris Oh, hell, I've got that as well now.
Gran Come up Elsie, will you?
Elsie (*to Tracy*) As I was saying, Sharon was there too, so I asked her if she'd lend you this. (*She takes out a wedding veil from the carrier bag*)
Tracy (*taking it*) Oh, Mam.
Idris (*bemused*) What's that?
Tracy It's a wedding veil. (*To Bobby*) Look, Bobby.
Gran You'll 'ave to change the bed.

Maisie enters from the kitchen

Maisie Finished with your cup Idris?

Elsie pushes Tracy out of the way as she advances towards Idris

Elsie (*furious*) What the hell is she doing here?
Idris (*now standing up*) Oh, my God!

Elsie physically attacks Idris and Tracy pulls her off. She turns to Maisie

Elsie I thought I told you never to come into my house again.
Maisie (*backing away*) I've only come to put things right.
Elsie You'd better get out before I bloody throw you out.

Elsie chases Maisie into the kitchen

Gran Will somebody come up and see to me? I've soaked the mattress.

Tracy It's my wedding veil, Dad.

Idris Your wedding veil? You're not getting married? You can't get married, you're too young.

Tracy What do you mean? Didn't Bobby tell you?

Bobby Course I told 'im.

Idris No you didn't. You only told me I had so long to live.

Bobby I never told you that.

Idris You mean I'm not going to die?

Tracy (*laughing*) You didn't think you were going to die, did you Dad?

Idris But I feel as if I'm going to die. What am I going to do now?

Gran It's all gone cold now.

Maisie runs out of the kitchen

Elsie (*off*) I'll give you five to get out.

She appears at the kitchen door and spots the breadknife which Tracy has left on the sideboard. She picks it up menacingly

One!

Maisie (*begging her*) Be reasonable.

Gran Tracy?

Elsie Two!

Maisie I've given him back his buttons.

Gran Bobby?

Elsie (*dodging between Tracy and Bobby*) Three!

Maisie Let's talk it over like sensible people.

Gran Idris?

Elsie Four!

Maisie (*running off*) Calm down!

Maisie runs off to the kitchen

Elsie (*following her*) Five!

Elsie follows her off

Idris (*looking at Tracy and the veil*) No ... no ... you can't get married ... you're too young.

Tracy (*shouting*) Too young? I'm pregnant.

Idris (*also shouting*) Pregnant?

There is a blood-curdling scream from the kitchen. Idris, Tracy and Bobby look towards the kitchen door

Maisie comes out carrying the breadknife which is dripping with blood

Maisie I only came to put things right.

She drops the knife. All four faint simultaneously

Black-out

CURTAIN

FURNITURE AND PROPERTY LIST

ACT I

On stage: *Living room*
Dining-table
3 dining chairs
Sideboard
2-seater settee
Armchair. *On it:* magazine for **Tracy**
Ironing board. *On it:* iron, item of clothing
Pile of ironed clothes
Basket of unironed clothes
Carpet

Bedroom
Bed with pillows and bedding. *Under pillow:* black hat
Small table. *On it:* dirty mugs, pack of playing cards, orange peel, clock,
    piggy bank
Chair. *On it:* handbag containing glasses
Orange for **Gran**

Hallway
Hallstand with mirror

Off stage: Plastic carrier containing knitting **(Jeffrey)**
Tray with 4 cups of tea, 1 cup cocoa **(Tracy)**
Cup of cocoa **(Tracy)**

Personal: **Idris:** glasses, watch (required throughout)

ACT II

Strike: *Living-room*
Ironing board, iron, clothing, basket
Tray, cups

Bedroom
Dirty mugs, orange peel

Set: *Living-room*
Bottles of whisky, gin, tonic, glasses in sideboard

Bedroom
Huge mallet under bedclothes

Re-set   *Bedroom*
Black hat under bedclothes
Pack of cards under pillow

Off stage: Tray with 2 cups of tea, 1 cup of cocoa, glass of Lucozade, 2 blue tablets
              (Tracy)
              Cup of cocoa **(Idris)**
              Magazine **(Maisie)**
              Magazine **(Bobby)**

Personal: **Idris:** crêpe bandage round head, 50p in pocket
            Tracy: watch
            Maisie: roller in hair, bottle of perfume in pocket

ACT III

Strike: *Living-room*
            Cups, glasses, gin bottle, Maisie's shoes and overall

            Bedroom
            Magazine

Set: *Living-room*
            Breadknife on sideboard
            Writing paper, pen on dining-table

Re-set: *Living-room*
            Tray on sideboard

            Bedroom
            Hat under bedclothes
            Tidy cards

Off stage: 2 cups of tea **(Tracy)**
             2 cups of tea **(Bobby)**
             Cup of tea **(Idris)**
             Plastic carrier bag containing wedding veil **(Elsie)**
             Breadknife dripping blood **(Maisie)**

Personal: **Idris:** surgical collar, glasses
            Maisie: 3 shirt buttons in pocket

LIGHTING PLOT

Property fittings required: pendants in living-room, hall and bedroom

Composite set: a living-room, a bedroom, a hallway.

ACT I Morning

To open: General interior light on all areas

Cue 1	**Tracy** (*after a slight pause*): "Oh, Gran." Loud clap of thunder *Several flashes of lightning*	(Page 11)
Cue 2	**Idris:** collapses in hall. Loud thunderclap *Black-out*	(Page 16)

ACT II Evening

To open: General interior light on all areas; pendants on

Cue 3	**Idris** trousers fall to his ankles and he faints *Black-out*	(Page 37)

ACT III Morning

To open: General interior lighting on all areas

Cue 4	**Maisie** drops the knife; all four faint simultaneously *Black-out*	(Page 53)

EFFECTS PLOT

ACT I

Cue 1   **Tracy** (*after a slight pause*): "Oh, Gran."   (Page 11)
            Loud clap of thunder

Cue 2   **Idris** collapses in hall   (Page 16)
            Loud thunderclap

ACT II

No cues

ACT III

Cue 3   **Idris:** "... a little faint, that's all."   (Page 46)
            Dishes smashing in kitchen, off

MADE AND PRINTED IN GREAT BRITAIN BY
LATIMER TREND & COMPANY LTD PLYMOUTH

MADE IN ENGLAND